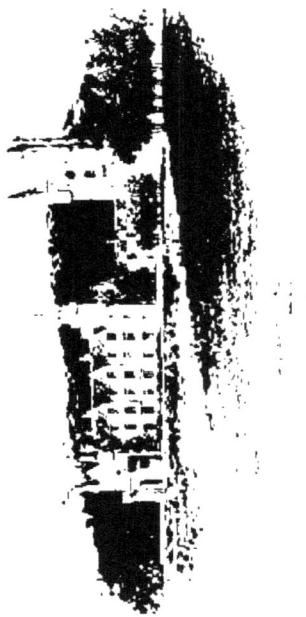

LEAVES

FROM THE JOURNAL

OF

OUR LIFE IN THE HIGHLANDS,

FROM 1848 TO 1861.

TO WHICH ARE PREFIXED AND ADDED EXTRACTS FROM THE SAME
JOURNAL GIVING AN ACCOUNT OF

EARLIER VISITS TO SCOTLAND,

AND TOURS IN ENGLAND AND IRELAND,

AND

YACHTING EXCURSIONS.

EDITED BY ARTHUR HELPS.

SECOND EDITION.

LONDON:
SMITH, ELDER AND CO.
1868.

TO

THE DEAR MEMORY OF HIM

WHO MADE THE LIFE OF THE WRITER BRIGHT AND HAPPY,

THESE SIMPLE RECORDS

ARE LOVINGLY AND GRATEFULLY INSCRIBED.

EDITOR'S PREFACE.

THE circumstances which have led to the publication of this Volume are, briefly, these.

During one of the Editor's official visits to Balmoral, her Majesty very kindly allowed him to see several extracts from her journal, relating to excursions in the Highlands of Scotland. He was much interested by them; and expressed the interest which he felt. It then occurred to her Majesty that these extracts, referring, as they did, to some of the happiest hours of her life, might be made into a book, to be printed privately, for presentation to members of the Royal Family and her Majesty's intimate friends; especially to those who had accompanied and attended her in these tours.

It was then suggested to her Majesty by some persons, among them a near and dear relative of the Queen, and afterwards by the Editor, that this work, if made known to others, would be very interesting to them as well as to the Royal Family and to her Majesty's intimate friends. The Queen, however, said, that she had no skill whatever in authorship; that these were, for the most part, mere homely accounts of excursions near home; and that she felt extremely reluctant to publish anything written by herself.

To this the Editor respectfully replied, that, if printed at all, however limited the impression, and however careful the selection of persons to whom copies might be given, some portions of the volume, or quite as probably incorrect representations of its contents, might find their way into the public journals. It would therefore, he thought, be better at once to place the volume within the reach of her Majesty's subjects, who would, no doubt, derive from it pleasure similar to that which it had afforded to the Editor himself. Moreover, it would be very gratifying to her subjects, who had always shown a sincere and ready sympathy with the personal joys and sorrows of their Sovereign,—to be allowed to know how her rare moments of leisure were passed in her Highland home, when every joy was heightened, and every care and sorrow diminished, by the loving companionship of the Prince Consort. With his memory the scenes to which this volume refers would always be associated.

Upon these considerations her Majesty eventually consented to its publication.

While the book was being printed, the Editor suggested that it would gain in interest if other extracts were added to it, describing her Majesty's progresses in England, Ireland, and the Channel Islands.

The Queen was pleased to assent; and the additions were accordingly made.

It will easily be seen that this little work does not make any pretension to be more than such a record of the impressions received by the Royal Author in the course of these journeys, as might hereafter serve to recall to her own mind the scenes and circumstances which had been the source of so much pleasure. All references to political questions, or to the affairs of Government, have, for obvious reasons, been studiously omitted. The book is mainly confined to the natural expressions of a mind rejoicing in the beauties of nature, and throwing itself, with a delight rendered keener by the rarity of its opportunities, into the enjoyment of a life removed, for the moment, from the pressure of public cares.

It would not be becoming in the Editor to dwell largely upon the merits of this work. He may, however, allude to the picturesque descriptions of scenery in which the work abounds; to the simplicity of diction throughout it; and to the perfect faithfulness of narration which is one of its chief characteristics; for in every page the writer describes what she thinks and feels, rather than what she might be expected to think and feel.

Moreover, he may point out the willingness to be pleased, upon which so much of the enjoyment of any tour depends : and also the exceeding kindliness of feeling—the gratitude even—with which the Royal Tourists recognize any attention paid to them, or any manifestation of the cordial attachment felt towards them, by any of her Majesty's subjects, from the highest to the humblest, whom they happen to meet with in the course of their journeys.

The Editor thinks that he should not be doing justice to the Royal Author's book—not doing what, if it were any other person's work which was entrusted to his editing, he should do—if he were to forbear giving utterance to the thoughts which occurred to him in reference to the notes to the Volume.

These notes, besides indicating that peculiar memory for persons, and that recognition of personal attachment, which have been very noticeable in our Sovereigns, illustrate, in a striking manner, the Patriarchal feeling (if one may apply such a word as "patriarchal" to a lady) which is so strong in the present occupant of the Throne. Perhaps there is no person in these realms who takes a more deep and abiding interest in the welfare of the household committed to his charge than our gracious Queen does in hers, or who feels more keenly what are the reciprocal duties of masters and servants.

Nor does any one wish more ardently than her Majesty, that there should be no abrupt severance of class from class, but rather a gradual blending together of all classes,—caused by a full community of interests, a constant interchange of good offices, and a kindly respect felt and expressed by each class to all its brethren in the great brotherhood that forms a nation.

Those whose duty it has been to attend upon the Queen in matters of business, must have noticed that her Majesty, as a person well versed in the conduct of affairs, is wont to keep closely to the point at issue, and to speak of nothing but what is directly connected with the matter before her. But whenever there is an exception to this rule, it arises from her Majesty's anxious desire to make some inquiry about the welfare of her subjects—to express her sympathy with this man's sorrow, or on that man's bereavement—to ask what is the latest intelligence about this disaster, or that suffering, and what can be done to remedy or assuage it—thus showing, unconsciously, that she is, indeed, the Mother of her People, taking the deepest interest in all that concerns them, without respect of persons, from the highest to the lowest.

The Editor thinks that one point of interest which will incidentally be disclosed by this publication, is the aspect of the Court in these our times. What would not the historian give to have similar materials within his reach, when writing about the reigns of the great Queen Elizabeth or the good Queen Anne ? There is always something in the present which has the appearance of being trivial and prosaic; but the future historian will delight in having details before him furnished by this book and by the *Life of the Prince Consort*,* which will enable him fully to describe the reign of Victoria, and justly to appreciate the private life of a Sovereign whose public life will enter so largely into the annals of the nineteenth century.

One more remark the Editor cannot refrain from making; namely, that it is evident that her Majesty never takes for granted the services and attentions which are rendered to her, and which we all know would be rendered to her from dutiful respect and regard, but views them as especial kindnesses shown to herself, and to which she makes no claim whatever from her exalted position as a Sovereign.

* A work which has met with a very cordial reception from the public, and which, from what the Editor has seen, will not by any means diminish in interest as it proceeds to describe the full and busy life of the Prince as a man.

(**xv**)

This latter trait, very characteristic of the Royal Author, gives, throughout, an additional charm to the book, which, on that account alone, and apart even from its many other merits, will, the Editor doubts not, be gratefully and affectionately welcomed by the public.

LONDON,
January, 1868.

CONTENTS.

CONTENTS.

Directions to the Binder.

EARLIER VISITS TO SCOTLAND.

First Visit to Scotland.

On Board the Royal George Yacht,
Monday, August 29, 1842.

AT five o'clock in the morning we left *Windsor*
for the railroad, the Duchess of Norfolk, Miss
Matilda Paget, General Wemyss, Colonel Bouverie, and Mr. Anson following us. Lord
Liverpool, Lord Morton, and Sir James Clark,
who also accompany us, had already gone on to
Woolwich.

We reached *London* at a quarter to six,
got into our carriages, and arrived at *Woolwich*
before seven. Albert and I immediately stepped
into our barge. There was a large crowd
to see us embark. The Duke of Cambridge,
Lord Jersey, Lord Haddington, Lord Bloomfield,
and Sir George Cockburn were present in full
uniform. Sir George handed me into the barge.

It was raining very hard when we got on board, and therefore we remained in our sitting-room.

I annex a list of our squadron :—

1. The ship " Pique," 36 guns.
2. The sloop " Daphne," 18 guns—(both of which join us at the *Nore*).
3. The steam-vessel " Salamander " (with the carriages on board).
4. The steam-vessel " Rhadamanthus " (Lord Liverpool and Lord Morton on board).
5. The steam-vessel " Monkey" Tender, which has towed us till nine o'clock (Mr. Anson and the equerries on board).
6. The steam-vessel " Shearwater," which is now towing us (Sir James Clark on board).
7. The steam-vessel " Black Eagle " (which has the ladies on board, and which tows us in front of the " Shearwater ").
8. The steam-vessel " Lightning " (with the Jäger Benda, and our two dogs, " Eôs " and " Cairnach," on board) in front, which has gone to take our barge on board from the " Pique."
9. The steam-vessel " Fearless " (for survey).

This composes our squadron, besides which the Trinity-House steamer goes with us, and, also, a packet. Innumerable little pleasure steamboats have been following us covered with people.

Tuesday, August 30.

We heard, to our great distress, that we had only gone 58 miles since eight o'clock last night. How annoying and provoking this is! We remained on deck all day lying on sofas; the sea was very rough towards evening, and I was very ill. We reached *Flamborough Head* on the Yorkshire coast by half-past five.

Wednesday, August 31.

At five o'clock in the morning we heard, to our great vexation, that we had only been going three knots an hour in the night, and were 50 miles from *St. Abb's Head.*

We passed *Coquet Island* and *Bamborough Castle* on the Northumberland coast, which I was unfortunately unable to see; but from my cabin I saw *Ferne Island*, with Grace Darling's light-

house on it; also *Rocky Islands* and *Holy Island*.
At half-past five I went on deck, and immediately lay down. We then came in sight of the
Scotch coast, which is very beautiful, so dark,
rocky, bold, and wild, totally unlike our coast.
We passed *St. Abb's Head* at half-past six.
Numbers of fishing-boats (in one of which was
a piper playing) and steamers full of people came
out to meet us, and on board of one large
steamer they danced a reel to a band. It was a
beautiful evening, calm, with a fine sunset, and the
air so pure.

One cannot help noticing how much longer the
days are here than they were in *England*. It
was not really dark till past eight o'clock, and on
Monday and Tuesday evening at *Windsor* it was
nearly dark by half-past seven, quite so before
eight. The men begged leave to dance, which they
did to the sound of a violin played by a little
sailor-boy; they also sang.

We remained on deck till twenty-five minutes
to nine, and saw many bonfires on the Scotch
coast — at *Dunbar* — Lord Haddington's place,
Tyninghame, and at other points on the coast.
We let off four rockets, and burned two blue

lights. It is surprising to see the sailors climb on the bowsprit and up to the top of the mast-head—this too at all times of the day and night. The man who carried the lantern to the main-top ran up with it in his mouth to the top. They are so handy and so well conducted.

We felt most thankful and happy that we were near our journey's end.

Thursday, September 1.

At a quarter to one o'clock, we heard the anchor let down—a welcome sound. At seven we went on deck, where we breakfasted. Close on one side were *Leith* and the high hills towering over *Edinburgh*, which was in fog; and on the other side was to be seen the *Isle of May* (where it is said Macduff held out against Macbeth), the *Bass Rock* being behind us. • At ten minutes past eight we arrived at *Granton Pier*, where we were met by the Duke of Buccleuch, Sir Robert Peel and others. They came on board to see us, and Sir Robert told us that the people were all in the highest good humour, though naturally a little disappointed at having waited for us yesterday.

We then stepped over a gangway on to the pier, the people cheering and the Duke saying that he begged to be allowed to welcome us. Our ladies and gentlemen had landed before us, safe and well, and we two got into a barouche, the ladies and gentlemen following. The Duke, the equerries, and Mr. Anson rode.

There were, however, not nearly so many people in *Edinburgh*, though the crowd and crush were such that one was really continually in fear of accidents. More regularity and order would have been preserved had there not been some mistake on the part of the Provost about giving due notice of our approach. The impression *Edinburgh* has made upon us is very great ; it is quite beautiful, totally unlike anything else I have seen ; and what is even more, Albert, who has seen so much, says it is unlike anything *he* ever saw ; it is so regular, everything built of massive stone, there is not a brick to be seen anywhere. The *High Street*, which is pretty steep, is very fine. Then the Castle, situated on that grand rock in the middle of the town, is most striking. On the other side the *Calton Hill*, with the *National Monument*, a building in the Grecian style ; *Nelson's Monu-*

ment ; Burns' Monument ; the *Gaol ;* the *National School,* &c. ; all magnificent buildings, and with *Arthur's Seat* in the background, overtopping the whole, form altogether a splendid spectacle. The enthusiasm was very great, and the people very friendly and kind. The Royal Archers Body Guard * met us and walked with us the whole way through the town. It is composed entirely of noblemen and gentlemen, and they all walked close by the carriage ; but were dreadfully pushed about. Amongst them were the Duke of Roxburgh and Lord Elcho on my side ; and Sir J. Hope on Albert's side. Lord Elcho† (whom I did not know at the time) pointed out the various monuments and places to me as we came along. When we were out of the town, we went faster. Every cottage is built of stone, and so are all the walls that are used as fences.

* The Duke of Buccleuch told me the other day, that the Archers Guard was established by James I., and was composed of men who were mounted and armed from head to foot, and who were bound always to be near the Sovereign's person. At Flodden Field, King James IV.'s body, it is said, was found covered and surrounded by the bodies of the Archers Guard.

† Now Earl of Wemyss.

The country and people have quite a different character from *England* and the English. The old women wear close caps, and all the children and girls are barefooted. I saw several handsome girls and children with long hair; indeed all the poor girls from sixteen and seventeen down to two or three years old, have loose flowing hair; a great deal of it red.

As we came along, we saw *Craigmillar Castle*, a ruin, where Mary, Queen of Scots, used to live. We reached *Dalkeith* at eleven; a large house, constructed of reddish stone, the greater part built by the Duchess of Monmouth, and the park is very fine and large. The house has three fronts, with the entrance on the left as you drive up. The Duchess of Buccleuch arrived directly after us, and we were shown up a very handsome staircase to our rooms, which are very comfortable. We both felt dreadfully tired and giddy.

We drove out together. The park is very extensive, with a beautiful view of *Arthur's Seat* and the *Pentland Hills;* and there is a pretty drive overhanging a deep valley. At eight we dined—a large party. Everybody was very kind and civil, and full of inquiries as to our voyage.

Dalkeith House,
Friday, September 2.

At breakfast I tasted the oatmeal porridge, which I think very good, and also some of the " Finnan haddies." We then walked out. The pleasure-grounds seem very extensive and beautiful, wild and hilly. We walked down along the stream (the river *Esk*), up a steep bank to a little cottage, and came home by the upper part of the walk. At four o'clock we drove out with the Duchess of Buccleuch and the Duchess of Norfolk —the Duke and equerries riding—the others in another carriage. We drove through *Dalkeith,* which was full of people, all running and cheering.

Albert says that many of the people look like Germans. The old women with that kind of cap which they call a " mutch," and the young girls and children with flowing hair, and many of them pretty, are very picturesque ; you hardly see any women with bonnets.

Such a thick " Scotch mist " came on that we were obliged to drive home through the village of *Lasswade,* and through Lord Melville's Park, which is very fine.

Saturday, September 3.

At ten o'clock we set off—we two in the barouche—all the others following, for *Edinburgh*. We drove in under *Arthur's Seat*, where the crowd began to be very great, and here the Guard of Royal Archers met us; Lord Elcho walking near me, and the Duke of Roxburgh and Sir J. Hope on Albert's side. We passed by *Holyrood Chapel*, which is very old and full of interest, and *Holyrood Palace*, a royal-looking old place. The procession moved through the *Old Town* up the *High Street*, which is a most extraordinary street from the immense height of the houses, most of them being eleven stories high, and different families living in each story. Every window was crammed full of people.

They showed us *Knox's House*, a curious old building, as is also the *Regent Murray's House*, which is in perfect preservation. In the *Old Town* the *High Church*, and *St. Paul's* in the *New Town,* are very fine buildings. At the barrier, the Provost presented us with the keys.

The girls of the *Orphan Asylum*, and the Trades in old costumes, were on a platform.

Further on was the *New Church*, to which—strange
to say, as the church is nearly finished—they
were going to lay the foundation stone. We at
length reached the Castle, to the top of which we
walked.

The view from both batteries is splendid,
like a panorama in extent. We saw from them
Heriot's Hospital, a beautiful old building, founded,
in the time of James, by a goldsmith and jeweller,
whom Sir Walter Scott has made famous in his
Fortunes of Nigel. After this, we got again into
the carriages and proceeded in the same way as
before, the pressure of the crowd being really quite
alarming ; and both I and Albert were quite terri-
fied for the Archers Guard, who had very hard
work of it ; but were of the greatest use. They
all carry a bow in one hand, and have their arrows
stuck through their belts.

Unfortunately, as soon as we were out of
Edinburgh, it began to rain, and continued raining
the whole afternoon without interruption. We
reached *Dalmeny*, Lord Roseberry's, at two o'clock.
The park is beautiful, with the trees growing down
to the sea. It commands a very fine view of
the *Forth*, the *Isle of May*, the *Bass Rock*, and

of *Edinburgh ;* but the mist rendered it almost impossible to see anything. The grounds are very extensive, being hill and dale and wood. The house is quite modern : Lord Roseberry built it, and it is very pretty and comfortable. We lunched there. The Roseberrys were all civility and attention. We left them about half-past three, and proceeded home through *Leith.*

The view of *Edinburgh* from the road before you enter *Leith* is quite enchanting ; it is, as Albert said, " fairy-like," and what you would only imagine as a thing to dream of, or to see in a picture. There was that beautiful large town, all of stone (no mingled colours of brick to mar it), with the bold Castle on one side, and the *Calton Hill* on the other, with those high sharp hills of *Arthur's Seat* and *Salisbury Crags* towering above all, and making the finest, boldest background imaginable. Albert said he felt sure the *Acropolis* could not be finer ; and I hear they sometimes call *Edinburgh* "the modern *Athens.*" The Archers Guard met us again at *Leith,* which is not a pretty town.

The people were most enthusiastic, and the crowd very great. The Porters all mounted, with curious Scotch caps, and their horses decorated with flowers, had a very singular effect ; but the fishwomen are the most striking-looking people, and are generally young and pretty women——very clean and very Dutch-looking, with their white caps and bright-coloured petticoats. They never marry out of their class.

At six we returned well tired.

Sunday, September 4.

We walked to see the new garden which is being made, and saw Mackintosh there, who was formerly gardener at *Claremont*. The view of *Dalkeith* (the village, or rather town) from thence is extremely picturesque, and Albert says very German-looking. We returned over a rough sort of bridge, made only of planks, which crosses the *Esk*, and which, with the wooded banks on each side, is excessively pretty. Received from Lady Lyttelton good accounts of our little children. At twelve o'clock there were prayers in the house, read by Mr. Ramsay, who also preached.

At half-past four the Duchess drove me out in her own phaeton, with a very pretty pair of chestnut ponies, Albert riding with the Duke and

Colonel Bouverie. We drove through parts of the park, through an old wood, and along the banks of the *South Esk* and the *North Esk*, which meet at a point from which there is such a beautiful view of the *Pentland Hills*. Then we drove, by a private road, to *Newbattle*, Lord Lothian's place. The park is very fine, and the house seems large ; we got out to look at a most magnificent beech-tree. The *South Esk* runs close before the house, by a richly wooded bank.

From thence we went to *Dalhousie*, Lord Dalhousie's. The house is a real old Scotch castle, of reddish stone. We got out for a moment, and the Dalhousies showed us the drawing-room. From the window you see a beautiful wooded valley, and a peep of the distant hills.

Lord Dalhousie said there had been no British sovereign there since Henry IV. We drove home by the same way that we came. The evening was—as the whole day had been—clear, bright, and frosty, and the *Moorfoot Hills* (another range) looked beautiful as we were returning. It was past seven when we got home.

Monday, September 5.

I held a Drawing-room at *Dalkeith* to-day, in the gallery. The Ministers and Scotch Officers of State were in the room, and the Royal Archers were in attendance in the room and outside of it, like the Gentlemen at Arms in *London*. Before the Drawing-room I received three addresses— from the Lord Provost and Magistrates, from the Scotch Church, and from the Universities of *St. Andrews, Glasgow*, and *Edinburgh*—to which I read answers. Albert received his just after I did mine, and read his answers beautifully.

Tuesday, September 6.

At nine o'clock we left *Dalkeith* as we came. It was a bright, clear, cold, frosty morning. As we drove along we saw the *Pentlands*, which looked beautiful, as did also *Arthur's Seat*, which we passed quite close by. The *Salisbury Crags*, too, are very high, bold, and sharp. Before this we saw *Craigmillar*. We passed through a back part of the town (which is most solidly built), close by *Heriot's Hospital*, and had a very fine view of the Castle.

I forgot to say that, when we visited the Castle, we saw the Regalia, which are very old and curious (they were lost for one hundred years); also the room in which James VI. of Scotland and the First of England was born—such a very, very small room, with an old prayer written on the wall. We had a beautiful view of *Edinburgh* and the *Forth*. At *Craigleith* (only a half-way house, nine miles) we changed horses. The Duke rode with us all the way as Lord Lieutenant of the county, until we arrived at *Dalmeny*, where Lord Hopetoun met us and rode with us. At eleven we reached the *South Queensferry*, where we got out of our carriage and embarked in a little steamer; the ladies and gentlemen and our carriages going in another. We went a little way up the *Forth*, to see *Hopetoun House*, Lord Hopetoun's, which is beautifully situated between *Hopetoun* and *Dalmeny*. We also saw *Dundas Castle*, belonging to Dundas of Dundas, and further on, beyond *Hopetoun*, *Blackness Castle*, famous in history. On the opposite side you see a square tower, close to the water, called *Rosyth*, where Oliver Cromwell's mother was said to have been born, and in the distance *Dunfermline*, where Robert Bruce is buried. We passed close by a very pretty island in the *Forth*, with an old castle on it, called *Inchgarvie*; and we could see the *Forth* winding beautifully, and had a distant glimpse of *Edinburgh* and its fine Castle. We landed safely on the other side at *North Queensferry*, and got into our carriages. Captain Wemyss, elder brother to General Wemyss, rode with us all the way beyond *Cowdenbeath* (eight miles). The first village we passed through on leaving the *Queensferry*, was *Inverkeithing*. We passed by Sir P. Durham's property.

We changed horses at *Cowdenbeath*. At a quarter-past one we entered *Kinross-shire*. Soon after, the country grew prettier, and the hills appeared again, partly wooded. We passed *Loch Leven*, and saw the castle on the lake from which poor Queen Mary escaped. There the country is rather flat, and the hills are only on one side. We changed horses next at *Kinross*. Soon after this, the mountains, which are rather barren, began to appear. Then we passed the valley of *Glen Farg;* the hills are very high on each side, and completely wooded down to the bottom of the valley, where a small stream runs on one side of the road—it is really lovely.

On leaving this valley you come upon a beautiful view of *Strathearn* and *Moncrieffe Hill.* We were then in *Perthshire.* We changed horses next at the *Bridge of Earn* (12 miles). At half-past three we reached *Dupplin*, Lord Kinnoull's. All the time the views of the hills, and dales, and streams were lovely. The last part of the road very bad travelling, up and down hill. *Dupplin* is a very fine modern house, with a very pretty view of the hills on one side, and a small waterfall close in front of the house. A battalion of the 42nd Highlanders was drawn up before the house, and the men looked very handsome in their kilts. We each received an address from the nobility and gentry of the county, read by Lord Kinnoull; and from the Provost and Magistrates of *Perth.* We then lunched. The Willoughbys, Kinnairds, Ruthvens, and Lord Mansfield, and one of his sisters, with others, were there. After luncheon, we walked a little way in the grounds, and then at five o'clock we set off again. We very soon came upon *Perth*, the situation of which is quite lovely; it is on the *Tay*, with wooded hills skirting it entirely on one side, and hills are seen again in the distance, the river winding beautifully.

Albert was charmed, and said it put him in mind of the situation of *Basle.* The town itself (which is very pretty) was immensely crowded, and the people very enthusiastic; triumphal arches had been erected in various places. The Provost presented me with the keys, and Albert with the freedom of the city. Two miles beyond is *Scone* (Lord Mansfield's), a fine-looking house of reddish stone.

Lord Mansfield and the Dowager Lady Mansfield received us at the door, and took us to our rooms, which were very nice.

Wednesday, September 7.

We walked out, and saw the mound on which the ancient Scotch kings were always crowned ; also the old arch with James VI.'s arms, and the old cross, which is very interesting.

Before our windows stands a sycamore-tree planted by James VI. A curious old book was brought to us from *Perth*, in which the last signatures are those of James I. (of England) and of Charles I., and we were asked to write our names in it, and we did so. Lord Mansfield told me yesterday that there were some people in the town who wore the identical dresses that had been worn in Charles I.'s time. At eleven o'clock we set off as before. We drove through part of *Perth*, and had a very fine view of *Scone*. A few miles on, we passed the field of battle of *Luncarty*, where tradition says the Danes were beaten by Lord Erroll's ancestor. We also passed Lord Lynedoch's property. We then changed horses at the " New Inn " at *Auchtergaven*. The *Grampians* came now distinctly into view ; they are indeed a grand range of mountains.

To the left we saw *Tullybugles*, where it is said the Druids used to sacrifice to Bel ; there are a few trees on the top of the mountain.

To the left ; but more immediately before us, we saw *Birnam*, where once stood *Birnam Wood*, so renowned in *Macbeth*. We passed a pretty shooting place of Sir W. Stewart's, called *Rohallion*, nearly at the foot of *Birnam*. To the right we saw the *Stormont* and *Strathtay*. Albert said, as we came along between the mountains, that to the right, where they were wooded, it was very like *Thüringen*, and on the left more like *Switzerland*. *Murthly*, to the right, which belongs to Sir W. Stewart, is in a very fine situation, with the *Tay* winding under the hill. This lovely scenery continues all along to *Dunkeld*. Lord Mansfield rode with us the whole way.

Just outside *Dunkeld*, before a triumphal arch, Lord Glenlyon's Highlanders, with halberds, met us, and formed our guard—a piper playing before us. *Dunkeld* is beautifully situated, in a narrow valley, on the banks of the *Tay*. We drove in to where the Highlanders were all drawn up, in the midst of their encampments, and where a tent was prepared for us to lunch in. Poor Lord Glenlyon* received us; but he had suddenly become totally blind, which is dreadful for him. He was led about by his wife; it was very melancholy. His blindness was caused by over-fatigue. The Dowager Lady Glenlyon, the Mansfields, Kinnoulls, Buccleuchs, and many others were there. We walked down the ranks of the Highlanders, and then partook of luncheon, the piper played, and one of the Highlanders † danced the "sword dance." (Two swords crossed are laid upon the ground, and the dancer has to dance across them

* The late Duke of Athole.

† Charles Christie, now steward to the present Dowager Duchess of Athole.

without touching them.) Some of the others danced a reel.

At a quarter to four we left *Dunkeld* as we came, the Highland Guard marching with us till we reached the outside of the town. The drive was quite beautiful all the way to *Taymouth.** The two highest hills of the range on each side are (to the right, as you go on after leaving *Dunkeld*) *Craig-y-Barns* and (to the left, imme-

---

* I revisited Taymouth last autumn, on the 3rd of October, from Dunkeld (incognita), with Louise, the Dowager Duchess of Athole, and Miss MacGregor. As we could not have driven through the grounds without asking permission, and we did not wish to be known, we decided upon not attempting to do so, and contented ourselves with getting out at a gate close to a small fort, into which we were led by a woman from the gardener's house, near to which we had stopped, and who had no idea who we were.

We got out, and looked from this height down upon the house below, the mist having cleared away sufficiently to show us everything; and then, unknown, quite in private, I gazed—not without deep emotion—on the scene of our reception twenty-four years ago, by dear Lord Breadalbane, in a princely style, not to be equalled in grandeur and poetic effect.

Albert and I were then only twenty-three, young and happy. How many are gone that were with us then!

I was very thankful to have seen it again.

It seemed unaltered.—1866.

diately above *Dunkeld*) *Craigvinean.* The *Tay*
winds along beautifully, and the hills are richly
wooded. We changed horses first at *Bala-
nagard* (nine miles), to which place Captain
Murray, Lord Glenlyon's brother, rode with us.
The hills grew higher and higher, and Albert
said it was very Swiss-looking in some parts.
High ribbed mountains appeared in the distance,
higher than any we have yet seen. This was
near *Aberfeldy* (nine miles), which is charmingly situated and the mountains very lofty.
At a quarter to six we reached *Taymouth.* At
the gate a guard of Highlanders, Lord Breadalbane's men, met us. *Taymouth* lies in a valley
surrounded by very high, wooded hills; it is
most beautiful. The house is a kind of castle,
built of granite. The *coup-d'œil* was indescrib-
able. There were a number of Lord Breadalbane's Highlanders, all in the Campbell tartan,
drawn up in front of the house, with Lord
Breadalbane himself in a Highland dress at their
head, a few of Sir Neil Menzies' men (in the
Menzies red and white tartan), a number of pipers
playing, and a company of the 92nd Highlanders,
also in kilts. The firing of the guns, the cheering

of the great crowd, the picturesqueness of the
dresses, the beauty of the surrounding country,
with its rich background of wooded hills, altogether
formed one of the finest scenes imaginable. It
seemed as if a great chieftain in olden feudal times
was receiving his sovereign. It was princely and
romantic. Lord and Lady Breadalbane took us
upstairs, the hall and stairs being lined with
Highlanders.

The Gothic staircase is of stone and very fine ;
the whole of the house is newly and exquisitely
furnished. The drawing-room, especially, is
splendid. Thence you go into a passage and
a library, which adjoins our private apartments.
They showed us two sets of apartments, and we
chose those which are on the right hand of the
corridor or ante-room to the library. At eight
we dined. Staying in the house, besides ourselves,
are the Buccleuchs and the two Ministers, the
Duchess of Sutherland and Lady Elizabeth Leveson Gower,* the Abercorns, Roxburghs, Kinnoulls,
Lord Lauderdale, Sir Anthony Maitland, Lord
Lorne,† the Fox Maules, Belhavens, Mr. and Mrs.

* Now Duchess of Argyll.

† The present Duke of Argyll.

William Russell, Sir J. and Lady Elizabeth, and the Misses Pringle, and two Messrs. Baillie, brothers of Lady Breadalbane. The dining-room is a fine room in Gothic style, and has never been dined in till this day. Our apartments also are inhabited for the first time. After dinner the grounds were most splendidly illuminated,—a whole chain of lamps along the railings, and on the ground was written in lamps, "Welcome Victoria—Albert."

A small fort, which is up in the woods, was illuminated, and bonfires were burning on the tops of the hills. I never saw anything so fairy-like. There were some pretty fireworks, and the whole ended by the Highlanders dancing reels, which they do to perfection, to the sound of the pipes, by torchlight, in front of the house. It had a wild and very gay effect.

Taymouth,
Thursday, September 8.

Albert went off at half-past nine o'clock to shoot with Lord Breadalbane. I walked out with the Duchess of Norfolk along a path overlooking the *Tay*, which is very clear, and ripples and foams along over the stones, the high mountains forming such a rich background. We got up to the dairy, which is a kind of Swiss cottage, built of quartz, very clean and nice. From the top of it there is a very pretty view of *Loch Tay*.

We returned home by the way we came. It rained the whole time, and very hard for a little while. Albert returned at half-past three. He had had excellent sport, and the trophies of it were spread out before the house—nineteen roe-deer, several hares and pheasants, and three brace of grouse; there was also a capercailzie that had been wounded, and which I saw afterwards, a magnificent large bird.

Albert had been near *Aberfeldy*, and had to shoot and walk the whole way back, Lord Breadalbane himself beating, and 300 Highlanders out. We went out at five, with Lady Breadalbane and the Duchess of Sutherland; we saw part of *Loch Tay*, and drove along the banks of the *Tay* under fine trees, and saw Lord Breadalbane's American buffaloes.

Friday, September 9.

Albert off again after nine o'clock, to shoot. Soon after he left I walked out with the Duchess of Norfolk across the iron bridge, and along a grass walk overhanging the *Tay.*

Two of the Highland Guard (they were stationed at almost every gate in the park) followed us, and it looked like olden times to see them with their swords drawn.

We then walked to a lodge on the same road. A fat, good-humoured little woman, about forty years old, cut some flowers for each of us, and the Duchess gave her some money, saying, "From Her Majesty." I never saw any one more surprised than she was; she, however, came up to me and said very warmly, that my people were delighted to see me in *Scotland.* It came on to rain very heavily soon afterwards, but we walked on. We saw a woman in the river, with her dress tucked up almost to her knees, washing potatoes.

The rain ceased just as we came home, but it went on pouring frequently. Albert returned at twenty minutes to three, having had very hard work on the moors, wading up to his knees in bogs every now and then, and had killed nine brace of grouse. We lunched; then we went to the drawing-room, and saw from the window the Highlanders dancing reels; but unfortunately it rained the whole time. There were nine pipers at the castle; sometimes one, and sometimes three played. They always played about breakfast-time, again during the morning, at luncheon, and also whenever we went in and out; again before dinner, and during most of dinner-time. We both have become quite fond of the bagpipes.

At a quarter-past five we drove out with the Duchess of Buccleuch and the Duchess of Sutherland (poor Lady Breadalbane not being very well), Lord Breadalbane riding the whole time before us. We took a most beautiful drive, first of all along part of the lake and between the hills—such thorough mountain scenery,—and with little huts, so low, so full of peat smoke, that one could hardly see anything for smoke. We saw *Ben Lawers*, which is said to be 4,000 feet high, very well, and further on, quite in the distance, *Ben More*—also the *Glenlyon*, and the river *Lyon*, and many fine glens. It was quite dark when we came home at half-past seven. At eight we dined; Lord and

Lady Ruthven and Lord and Lady Duncan dined here. After dinner came a number of people, about ninety, and there was a ball. It opened with a quadrille, which I danced with Lord Breadalbane, and Albert with the Duchess of Buccleuch. A number of reels were danced, which it was very amusing and pretty to see.

Saturday, September 10.

We walked to the dairy and back—a fine bright morning; the weather the two preceding days had been very unfortunate. I drove a little way with Lady Breadalbane, the others walking, and then got out, and each of us planted two trees, a fir and an oak. We got in again, and drove with the whole party down to the lake, where we embarked. Lady Breadalbane, the Duchess of Sutherland and Lady Elizabeth went by land, but all the others went in boats. With us were Lord Breadalbane and the Duchess of Norfolk and Duchess of Buccleuch; and two pipers sat on the bow and played very often. I have since been reading in *The Lady of*·

the Lake, and this passage reminds me of our voyage :—

> " See the proud pipers on the bow,
> And mark the gaudy streamers flow
> From their loud chanters down, and sweep
> The furrow'd bosom of the deep,
> As, rushing through the lake amain,
> They plied the ancient Highland strain."

Our row of 16 miles up *Loch Tay* to *Auch-more,* a cottage of Lord Breadalbane's, near the end of the lake, was the prettiest thing imaginable. We saw the splendid scenery to such great advantage on both sides : *Ben Lawers,* with small waterfalls descending its sides, amid other high mountains wooded here and there ; with *Kenmore* in the distance ; the view, looking back, as the loch winds, was most beautiful. The boatmen sang two Gaelic boat-songs, very wild and singular ; the language so guttural and yet so soft. Captain McDougall, who steered, and who is the head of the McDougalls, showed us the real " brooch of Lorn," which was taken by his ancestor from Robert Bruce in a battle. The situation of *Auch-more* is exquisite ; the trees growing so beautifully down from the top of the mountains, quite into the water, and the mountains all round, make it an enchanting spot. We landed and lunched in the cottage, which is a very nice little place. The day was very fine; the Highlanders were there again. We left *Auchmore* at twenty minutes past three, having arrived there at a quarter before three. The kindness and attention to us of Lord and of Lady Breadalbane (who is very delicate) were unbounded. We passed *Killin*, where there is a mountain stream running over large stones, and forming waterfalls.

The country we came to now was very wild, beginning at *Glen Dochart*, through which the *Dochart* flows; nothing but moors and very high rocky mountains. We came to a small lake called, I think, *Laragilly*, amidst the wildest and finest scenery we had yet seen. *Glen Ogle*, which is a sort of long pass, putting one in mind of the prints of the *Kyber Pass*, the road going for some way down hill and up hill, through these very high mountains, and the escort in front looking like mere specks from the great height. We also saw *Ben Voirlich*. At *Loch Earn Head* we changed horses. Lord Breadalbane rode with us the whole way up to this point, and then he put his

Factor (in Highland dress) up behind our carriage. It came on to rain, and rained almost the whole of the rest of the time. We passed along *Loch Earn*, which is a very beautiful long lake skirted by high mountains ; but is not so long or so large as *Loch Tay*. Just as we turned and went by *St. Fillans*, the view of the lake was very fine. There is a large detached rock with rich verdure on it, which is very striking.

We also saw *Glenartney*, the mountain on which Lord Willoughby has his deer forest. We passed by Sir D. Dundas's place, *Dunira*, before we changed horses at *Comrie*, for the last time, and then by Mr. Williamson's, and by *Ochtertyre*, Sir W. Keith Murray's.

Triumphal arches were erected in many places. We passed through *Crieff*, and a little past seven reached *Drummond Castle*, by a very steep ascent. Lord Willoughby received us at the door, and showed us to our rooms, which are small but nice. Besides Lord and Lady Willoughby and the two Misses Willoughby, and our own people, the dinner-party was composed of the Duchess of Sutherland and Lady Elizabeth L. Gower, Lord and Lady Carington, Mr. and Mrs. Heathcote, the Duke de Richelieu, Lord Ossulston, Mr. Drummond, and the officers of the Guard.

Drummond Castle,
Sunday, September 11.

We walked in the garden, which is really very fine, with terraces, like an old French garden. Part of the old castle and the archway remains.

At twelve o'clock we had prayers in the drawing-room, which were read by a young clergyman, who preached a good sermon.

It poured the whole afternoon, and, after writing, I read to Albert the three first cantos of *The Lay of the Last Minstrel,* which delighted us both; and then we looked over some curious, fine old prints by Ridinger. At eight we dined. The Duchess of Sutherland and Lady Elizabeth had gone; but Lord and Lady Abercorn and Lord and Lady Kinnoull and their daughter added to the party.

Monday, September 12.

Albert got up at five o'clock to go out deer-stalking. I walked out with the Duchess of Norfolk.

All the Highlanders (Lord Willoughby's people, 110 in number), were drawn up in the court, young Mr. Willoughby and Major Drummond being at their head, and I walked round with Lady Willoughby. All the arms they wore belonged to Lord Willoughby ; and there was one double-hilted sword, which had been at the battle of *Bannockburn.* I hear that at *Dunkeld* there were nearly 900 Highlanders, 500 being *Athole* men ; and, altogether, with the various Highlanders who were on guard, there were 1,000 men.

At length—a little before three—to my joy, Albert returned, dreadfully sunburnt, and a good deal tired ; he had shot a stag. He said the exertion and difficulty were very great. He had changed his dress at a small farm-house. *Glenartney* is ten miles from *Drummond Castle;* he drove there. Campbell of Monzie (pronounced " Monie "), a young gentleman who has a place near here, went with him and was, Albert said, extremely active. To give some description of this curious sport, I will copy an extract from a letter Albert has written to Charles,* giving a short account of it :—

" Without doubt deer-stalking is one of the " most fatiguing, but it is also one of the most inte- " resting of pursuits. There is not a tree, or a " bush behind which you can hide yourself. . . " One has, therefore, to be constantly on the alert " in order to circumvent them ; and to keep under " the hill out of their wind, crawling on hands " and knees, and dressed entirely in grey."

At half-past four we drove out with Lady Willoughby and the Duchess of Buccleuch. We drove through *Fern Tower* (belonging to the widow of the first Sir D. Baird), where we stopped the carriage ; then to *Abercairny*, Major Moray's. We got out there a moment to look at the very fine house he is building, then drove home by *Monzie* (Campbell of Monzie's), and Sir W. Murray's, and had a very good view of the Highland hills— a very fine day. At eight we dined. The Belhavens, Seftons, Cravens, Campbell of Monzie, and various others composed the party. After dinner more people came—several in kilts ; and

* My half-brother, Prince Leiningen, who died in 1856.

many reels were danced; Campbell of Monzie is an exceedingly good dancer. We danced one country dance—I with Lord Willoughby—and Albert with Lady Carington.

Tuesday, September 13.

We had to start early, and therefore got up soon after seven o'clock; breakfast before eight. At nine we set off. The morning was very foggy and hazy. We passed near Lord Strathallan's place and stopped for a moment where old Lady Strathallan was seated. Lord Willoughby rode with us the whole way till we arrived here. Soon after this we came to a very extraordinary Roman encampment at *Ardoch*, called the "Lindrum." Albert got out; but I remained in the carriage, and Major Moray showed it to him. They say it is one of the most perfect in existence.

We changed horses at *Greenloaning*, and passed through *Dunblane*. At twelve o'clock we reached *Stirling*, where the crowd was quite fearful, and the streets so narrow, that it was most alarming; and order was not very well kept. Up to the Castle, the road or street is dreadfully steep;

we had a foot procession before us the whole
way, and the heat was intense. The situation
of the Castle is extremely grand ; but I prefer that
of *Edinburgh Castle.* Old Sir Archibald Christie
explained everything to us very well. We were
shown the room where James II. killed Douglas,
and the window out of which he was thrown. The
ceiling is most curious. A skeleton was found
in the garden only twenty-five years ago, and there
appears to be little doubt it was Douglas's. From
the terrace the view is very extensive ; but it was
so thick and hazy, that we could not see the Highland hills well. Sir A. Christie showed us the field
of the battle of *Bannockburn ;* and the "Knoll,"
close under the walls of the Castle, from which
the ladies used to watch the tournaments; all
the embankments yet remain. We also saw
Knox's pulpit.

We next passed through *Falkirk*, and changed
horses at *Callander Park*, Mr. Forbes's ; both he
and Sir Michael Bruce having ridden with us
from beyond *Stirling.* We passed Lord Zetland
on the road, and shortly before reaching *Linlithgow,*
where we changed horses, Lord Hopetoun met
us. Unfortunately, we did not see the Palace,

which, I am told, is well worth seeing. The Duke of Buccleuch met us soon after this, and, accompanied by a large number of his tenants, rode with us on horseback to *Dalkeith.* We changed horses at *Kirkliston,* and lastly at the outskirts of *Edinburgh.* There were a good many people assembled at *Edinburgh;* but we were unable to stop. We reached *Dalkeith* at half-past five.

The journey was 65 miles, and I was very tired, and felt most happy that we had safely arrived here.

Dalkeith,
Wednesday, September 14.

This is our last day in *Scotland;* it is really a delightful country, and I am very sorry to leave it. We walked out and saw the fine greenhouse the Duke has built, all in stone, in the Renaissance style. At half-past three o'clock we went out with the Duchess of Buccleuch, only Colonel Bouverie riding with us. We drove through *Melville Park,* and through one of the little collier villages (of which there are a great many about *Dalkeith*), called *Loanhead,* to *Rosslyn.*

We got out at the chapel, which is in excellent

preservation ; it was built in the fifteenth century, and the architecture is exceedingly rich. It is the burying place of the family of Lord Rosslyn, who keeps it in repair. Twenty Barons of Rosslyn are buried there in armour. A great crowd had collected about the chapel when we came out of it.

From *Rosslyn* we then drove to *Hawthornden*, which is also beautifully situated at a great height above the river. To our great surprise we found an immense crowd of people there, who must have run over from *Rosslyn* to meet us.

We got out, and went down into some of the very curious caves in the solid rock, where Sir Alexander Ramsay and his brave followers concealed themselves, and held out for so long a time. The Duchess told us there were many of these caves all along the river to *Rosslyn*.

We came home through *Bonnyrigg*, another collier village, and through *Dalkeith*.

Thursday, September 15.

We breakfasted at half-past seven o'clock, and at eight we set off, with the Duchess of Buccleuch, Lord Liverpool and Lord Hardwicke following. The ladies and equerries had embarked earlier. The day was very bright and fine. The arrangements in *Edinburgh*, through which we had to pass, were extremely well managed, and excellent order was kept. We got out of the carriage on the pier, and went at once on board the " Trident," a large steamboat belonging to the General Steam Navigation Company. The Duke and Duchess of Buccleuch, Lady J. Scott, the Emlyns, Lord Cawdor, and Lady M. Campbell, came on board with us, and we then took leave of them. We both thanked the Duke and Duchess for their extreme kindness, attention, and hospitality to us, which really were very great— indeed we had felt ourselves quite at home at *Dalkeith*.

As the fair shores of *Scotland* receded more and more from our view, we felt quite sad that this very pleasant and interesting tour was over ; but we shall never forget it.

On board the " Trident " (where the accommodation for us was much larger and better than on board the " Royal George," and which was beautifully fitted up,) were Admiral Sir E. Bruce, a pleasant old man, Commander Bullock, and three other officers. The "Rhadamanthus," with some servants and carriages, set off last night, as well as the " Shearwater," with Lord Liverpool and Lord Hardwicke on board.

The " Salamander " (with Mr. and Mrs. Anson on board), the " Fearless," and the " Royal George" yacht set off at the same time with us, but the wind being against us, we soon lost sight of the yacht, and, not very long after, of all our steamers, except the " Monarch," which belongs to the General Steam Navigation Company, and had some of our horses on board. It started nearly at the same time, and was the only one which could keep up with us. We passed *Tantallon Castle*, a grand old ruin on the coast, and quite close to the *Bass Rock*, which is very fine, and nearly opposite *Tantallon*. It was entirely covered with sea-gulls and island geese, which swarm in thousands and thousands, quite whitening its sides, and hovering above and around it.

At two o'clock we passed the famed *St. Abb's Head*, which we had so longed to see on our first voyage to *Scotland*. I read a few stanzas out of *Marmion*, giving an account of the voyage of the nuns to *Holy Island*, and saw the ruins of the convent on it; then *Bamborough Castle*, and a little further on the *Ferne Islands*. We were very sorry to hear that poor Grace Darling had died the night before we passed the first time.

Friday, September 16.

We heard that we had passed *Flamborough Head* at half-past five in the morning. The "Black Eagle" we passed at half-past eight last night, and we could only just see her smoke by the time we came on deck. At half-past nine I followed Albert on deck; it was a fine, bright morning. We had some coffee, and walked about; we were then quite in the open sea; it was very fine all day. At five we were close to the "Rhadamanthus," which had been in sight all day. We had a very pleasant little dinner on deck, in a small tent made of flags, at half-past five. We passed *Yarmouth* at about a quarter to six—very flat—and looking, Albert said, like a Flemish town. We walked up and down on deck, admiring the splendid moonlight, which was reflected so beautifully on the sea.

We went below at half-past seven, and I read

the fourth and fifth cantos of *The Lay of the Last Minstrel* to Albert, and then we played on the piano.

Saturday, September 17.

At three o'clock in the morning we were awakened by loud guns, which, however, were welcome sounds to us, as we knew that we were at the *Nore*, the entrance of the river.   About six we heard the " Rhadamanthus " had just passed us, and they said we were lying off *Southend*, in order to let the " Black Eagle " come up.   It was a very bright day, though a little hazy.

The shipping in the river looked very pretty as we passed along.   At ten minutes past ten we got into the barge and landed.   The Duchess of Norfolk and Miss Matilda Paget and the equerries were all there, but the others we knew nothing of.   Sir James Clark had been on board the " Trident " with us.   We drove off at once to the railway terminus, and reached *Windsor Castle* at half-past twelve o'clock.

VISIT TO BLAIR ATHOLE.

Monday, September 9, 1844.

We got up at a quarter to six o'clock. We breakfasted. Mama came to take leave of us; Alice and the baby * were brought in, poor little things, to wish us "good-by." Then good Bertie† came down to see us, and Vicky‡ appeared as "voyageuse," and was all impatience to go. At seven we set off with her for the railroad, Viscountess Canning and Lady Caroline Cocks § in our carriage. A very wet morning. We got into the carriage again at *Paddington*, and proceeded to *Woolwich*, which we reached at nine. Vicky was safely put into the boat, and then care-

* Prince Alfred, then only five weeks old.

† Name by which the Prince of Wales is always called in his family.

‡ Victoria, Princess Royal.

§ Now Lady C. Courtenay.

fully carried on deck of the yacht by Renwick,* the sergeant-footman, whom we took with us in the boat on purpose. Lord Liverpool, Lord Aberdeen, and Sir James Clark met us on board. Sir Robert Peel was to have gone with us, but could not, in consequence of his little girl being very ill.

Blair Athole,
Wednesday, September 11.

At six o'clock we inquired and heard that we were in the port of *Dundee.* Albert saw our other gentlemen, who had had a very bad passage. Tuesday night they had a dreadful storm. *Dundee* is a very large place, and the port is large and open ; the situation of the town is very fine, but the town itself is not so. The Provost and people had come on board, and wanted us to land later, but we got this satisfactorily arranged. At half-past eight we got into our barge with Vicky, and our ladies and gentlemen. The sea was bright and blue ; the boat danced along beautifully. We had about a quarter of a mile to row.

* Now pensioned : promoted to Gentleman Porter in 1854. A very good servant ; and a native of Galashiels.

A staircase, covered with red cloth, was arranged for us to land upon, and there were a great many people; but everything was so well managed that all crowding was avoided, and only the Magistrates were below the platform where the people were. Albert walked up the steps with me, I holding his arm and Vicky his hand, amidst the loud cheers of the people, all the way to the carriage, our dear Vicky behaving like a grown-up person—not put out,. nor frightened, nor nervous. We got into our postchaise, and at the same time Renwick took Vicky up in his arms and put her in the next carriage with her governess and nurse.

There was a great crowd in *Dundee*, but everything was very well managed, and there would have been no crowding at all, had not, as usual, about twenty people begun to run along with the carriage, and thus forced a number of others to follow. About three miles beyond *Dundee* we stopped at the gate of Lord Camperdown's place: here a triumphal arch had been erected, and Lady Camperdown and Lady Duncan and her little boy, with others, were all waiting to welcome us, and were very civil and kind. The little boy, beautifully dressed in the Highland dress, was carried to

Vicky, and gave her a basket with fruit and flowers. I said to Albert I could hardly believe that our child was travelling with us—it put me so in mind of myself when I was the "little Princess." Albert observed that it was always said that parents lived their lives over again in their children, which is a very pleasant feeling.

The country from here to *Cupar Angus* is very well cultivated, and you see hills in the distance. The harvest is only now being got in, but is very good ; and everything much greener than in *England*. Nothing could be quieter than our journey, and the scenery is so beautiful! It is very different from *England:* all the houses built of stone ; the people so different,—sandy hair, high cheek-bones ; children with long shaggy hair and bare legs and feet ; little boys in kilts. Near *Dunkeld*, and also as you get more into the *Highlands*, there are prettier faces. Those jackets which the girls wear are so pretty ; all the men and women, as well as the children, look very healthy.

Cupar Angus is a small place—a village— 14 miles from *Dundee*. There you enter *Perthshire*. We crossed the river *Isla*, which made me think of my poor little dog "Isla." For about five or six miles we went along a very pretty but rough cross-road, with the *Grampians* in the distance. We saw *Birnam Wood* and Sir W. Stewart's place in that fine valley on the opposite side of the river. All along such splendid scenery, and Albert enjoyed it so much —rejoicing in the beauties of nature, the sight of mountains, and the pure air.

The peeps of *Dunkeld*, with the river *Tay* deep in the bottom, and the view of the bridge and cathedral, surrounded by the high wooded hills, as you approached it, were lovely in the extreme. We got out at an inn (which was small, but very clean) at *Dunkeld*, and stopped to let Vicky have some broth. Such a charming view from the window! Vicky stood and bowed to the people out of the window. There never was such a good traveller as she is, sleeping in the carriage at her usual times, not put out, not frightened at noise or crowds ; but pleased and amused. She never heard the anchor go at night on board ship ; but slept as sound as a top.

Shortly after leaving *Dunkeld*, which is 20 miles from *Blair*, and 15 from *Cupar Angus*, we met Lord Glenlyon in a carriage ; he jumped out and rode with us the whole way to *Blair*,—and a most beautiful road it is. Six miles on, in the woods to the left, we could see *Kinnaird House*, where the late Lady Glenlyon (Lord Glenlyon's mother, who died about two or three months ago) used to live. Then we passed the point of *Logierait*, where there are the remains of an ancient castle,— the old Regality Court of the Dukes of Athole. At *Moulinearn* we tasted some of the "*Athole* brose," which was brought to the carriage.

We passed *Pitlochrie*, a small village, *Faskally*, a very pretty place of Mr. Butter's, to the left, and then came to the *Pass of Killiecrankie*, which is quite magnificent; the road winds along it, and you look down a great height, all wooded on both sides; the *Garry* rolling below it. I cannot describe how beautiful it is. Albert was in perfect ecstasies. *Lude*, Mr. Mc Inroy's, to the right, is very pretty. *Blair Athole* is only four or five miles from the *Killiecrankie Pass*. Lord Glenlyon has had a new approach made. The house is a large plain white building, surrounded by high hills, which one can see from the windows. Lord and Lady Glenlyon, with their little boy, received us at the door, and showed us to our rooms, and then left us.

Blair Castle, Blair Athole,
Thursday, September 12.

We took a delightful walk of two hours.
Immediately near the house the scenery is very
wild, which is most enjoyable. The moment
you step out of the house you see those splendid
hills all round. We went to the left through
some neglected pleasure - grounds, and then
through the wood, along a steep winding path
overhanging the rapid stream. These Scotch
streams, full of stones, and clear as glass, are most
beautiful; the peeps between the trees, the depth
of the shadows, the mossy stones, mixed with
slate, &c., which cover the banks, are lovely; at
every turn you have a picture. We were up high,
but could not get to the top; Albert in such
delight; it is a happiness to see him, he is in such
spirits. We came back by a higher drive, and
then went to the Factor's house, still higher
up, where Lord and Lady Glenlyon are living,
having given *Blair* up to us. We walked on, to
a corn-field where a number of women were
cutting and reaping the oats ("shearing" as they

call it in *Scotland*), with a splendid view of the hills before us, so rural and romantic, so unlike our daily *Windsor* walk (delightful as that is) ; and this change does such good : as Albert observes, it refreshes one for a long time. We then went into the kitchen-garden, and to a walk from which there is a magnificent view. This mixture of great wildness and art is perfection.

At a little before four o'clock Albert drove me out in the pony phaeton till nearly six—such a drive! Really to be able to sit in one's pony carriage, and to see such wild, beautiful scenery as we did, the farthest point being only five miles from the house, is an immense delight. We drove along *Glen Tilt*, through a wood overhanging the river *Tilt*, which joins the *Garry*, and as we left the wood we came upon such a lovely view, —*Ben-y-Ghlo* straight before us—and under these high hills the river *Tilt* gushing and winding over stones and slates, and the hills and mountains skirted at the bottom with beautiful trees ; the whole lit up by the sun ; and the air so pure and fine ; but no description can at all do it justice, or give an idea of what this drive was.

Oh ! what can equal the beauties of nature !

What enjoyment there is in them! Albert enjoys it so much; he is in ecstasies here. He has inherited this love for nature from his dear father.

We went as far as the *Marble Lodge*, a keeper's cottage, and came back the same way.

Monday, September 16.

After our luncheon at half-past three, Albert drove me (Lord Glenlyon riding with us) to the *Falls of the Bruar*. We got out at the road, and walked to the upper falls, and down again by the path on the opposite side. It is a walk of three miles round, and a very steep ascent; at every turn the view of the rushing falls is extremely fine, and looking back on the hills, which were so clear and so beautifully lit up, with the rapid stream below, was most exquisite. We threw stones down to see the effect in the water. The trees which surround the falls were planted by the late Duke of Athole in compliance with Burns's "*Petition*." *

The evening was beautiful, and we feasted our

* *The Humble Petition of Bruar Water to the Noble Duke of Athole.*

eyes on the ever-changing, splendid views of the hills and vales as we drove back. Albert said that the chief beauty of mountain scenery consisted in its frequent changes. We came home at six o'clock.

Tuesday, September 17.

At a quarter to four o'clock we drove out, Albert driving me, and the ladies and Lord Glenlyon following in another carriage. We drove to the *Pass of Killiecrankie*, which looked in its greatest beauty and splendour, and appeared quite closed, so that one could not imagine how one was to get out of it. We drove over a bridge to the right, where the view of the pass both ways, with the *Garry* below, is beautiful. We got out a little way beyond this and walked on a mile to the *Falls of the Tummel*, the stream of which is famous for salmon; these falls, however, are not so fine, or nearly so high, as those of the *Bruar*. We got home at half-past six; the day was fast fading, and the lights were lovely.

We watched two stags fighting just under our window; they are in an enclosure, and roar incessantly.

Wednesday, September 18.

At nine o'clock we set off on ponies, to go up one of the hills, Albert riding the dun pony and I the grey, attended only by Lord Glenlyon's excellent servant, Sandy Mc Ara, in his Highland dress. We went out by the back way across the road, and to the left through the ford, Sandy leading my pony and Albert following closely, the water reaching up above Sandy's knees. We then went up the hill of *Tulloch*, first straight up a very steep cabbage-field, and then in a zigzag manner round, till we got up to the top; the ponies scrambling up over stones and everything, and never making a false step; and the view all round being splendid and most beautifully lit up. We went up to the very highest top, which cannot be seen from the house or from below; and from here the view is like a panorama : you see the *Falls of the Bruar, Ben-y-Chat, Ben Vrackie, Ben-y-Ghlo*, the *Killiecrankie Pass*, and a whole range of distant hills on the other side, which one cannot at all see from below. In the direction of *Taymouth* you also see *Dalnacardoch*, the first stage from *Blair*. *Blair* itself and the houses in the village looked like little toys from the great height we were on. It was quite romantic. Here we were with only this Highlander behind us holding the ponies (for we got off twice and walked about)—not a house, not a creature near us, but the pretty Highland sheep, with their horns and black faces,—up at the top of *Tulloch*, surrounded by beautiful mountains.

We came back the same way that we went, and stopped at the ford to let the ponies drink before we rode through. We walked from inside the gate, and came home at half-past eleven,— the most delightful, most romantic ride and walk I ever had. I had never been up such a mountain, and then the day was so fine. The hill of *Tulloch* is covered with grass, and is so delightfully soft to walk upon.

Thursday, September 19.

Albert set off, immediately after luncheon, deerstalking, and I was to follow and wait below in order to see the deer driven down. At four o'clock I set off with Lady Glenlyon and Lady

Canning, Mr. Oswald and Lord Charles Wellesley
riding, by the lower *Glen Tilt* drive. We stopped
at the end; but were still in the wood; Sandy was
looking out and watching. After waiting we were
allowed to come out of the carriage, and came
upon the road, where we saw some deer on the
brow of the hill. We sat down on the ground,
Lady Canning and I sketching, and Sandy and
Mr. Oswald, both in Highland costume, (the same
that they all wear here, viz. a grey cloth jacket
and waistcoat, with a kilt and a Highland bonnet,)
lying on the grass and looking through glasses.
After waiting again some time, we were told in a
mysterious whisper that "they were coming," and
indeed a great herd *did* appear on the brow of the
hill, and came running down a good way, when
most provokingly two men who were walking on
the road—which they had no business to have done
—suddenly came in sight, and then the herd all
ran back again and the sport was spoilt. After
waiting some little while we observed Albert, Lord
Glenlyon, and the keepers on the brow of the hill,
and we got into the carriage, drove a little way,
went over the bridge, where there is a shepherd's
" shiel," and got out and waited for them to join

us, which they did almost immediately,—looking very picturesque with their rifles. My poor Albert had not even fired one shot for fear of spoiling the whole thing, but had been running about a good deal. The group of keepers and dogs was very pretty. After talking and waiting a little while, we walked some way on, and then Albert drove home with us.

Saturday, September 21.

After breakfast Albert saw Lord Glenlyon, who proposed that he should go deer-stalking and that I should follow him. At twenty minutes to eleven we drove off with Lady Canning for *Glen Tilt*. The day was glorious and it would have been a pity to lose it, but it was a long hard day's work, though extremely delightful and enjoyable, and unlike anything I had ever done before. I should have enjoyed it still more had I been able to be with Albert the whole time.

We drove nearly to Peter Fraser's house, which is between the *Marble Lodge* and *Forest Lodge*. Here Albert and I walked about a little, and then Lady Canning and we mounted our ponies

and set off on our journey, Lord Glenlyon leading
my pony the whole way, Peter Fraser, the head-
keeper (a wonderfully active man) leading the
way; Sandy and six other Highlanders carrying
rifles and leading dogs, and the rear brought up
by two ponies with our luncheon-box. Lawley,*
Albert's Jäger, was also there, carrying one of
Albert's rifles; the other Albert slung over his
right shoulder, to relieve Lawley. So we set off
and wound round and round the hill, which had
the most picturesque effect imaginable. Such a
splendid view all round, finer and more extensive
the higher we went! The day was delightful;
but the sun very hot. We saw the highest point of
Ben-y-Ghlo, which one cannot see from below, and
the distant range of hills we had seen from *Tulloch*
was beautifully softened by the slightest haze. We
saw *Loch Vach*. The road was very good, and
as we ascended we had to speak in a whisper,
as indeed we did almost all day, for fear of coming
upon deer unawares. The wind was, however,
right, which is everything here for the deer. I

* A very good man. His health obliged him to give up
being a Jäger in 1848; he was then appointed a Page, in which
position he continued till he died, in November, 1865.

wish we could have had Landseer with us to sketch our party, with the background, it was so pretty, as were also the various " halts," &c. If I only had had time to sketch them !

We stopped at the top of the *Chrianan*, whence you look down an immense height. It is here that the eagles sometimes sit. Albert got off and looked about in great admiration, and walked on a little, and then remounted his pony. We then went nearly to the top of *Cairn Chlamain*, and here we separated, Albert going off with Peter, Lawley, and two other keepers, to get a " quiet shot " as they call it ; and Lady Canning, Lord Glenlyon, and I went up quite to the top, which is deep in moss. Here we sat down and stayed some time sketching the ponies below ; Lord Glenlyon and Sandy remaining near us. The view was quite beautiful, nothing but mountains all around us, and the solitude, the complete solitude, very impressive. We saw the range of *Mar Forest*, and the inner range to the left, receding from us, as we sat facing the hill, called *Scarsach*, where the counties of *Perth, Aberdeen*, and *Inverness* join. My pony was brought up for me, and we then descended this highest pinnacle, and proceeded on a level to meet Albert, whom I descried coming towards us. We met him shortly after; he had had bad luck, I am sorry to say. We then sat down on the grass and had some luncheon; then I walked a little with Albert and we got on our ponies. As we went on towards home some deer were seen in *Glen Chroime,* which is called the "Sanctum;" where it is supposed that there are a great many. Albert went off soon after this, and we remained on *Sron a Chro,* for an hour, I am sure, as Lord Glenlyon said by so doing we should turn the deer to Albert, whereas if we went on we should disturb and spoil the whole thing. So we submitted. Albert looked like a little speck creeping about on an opposite hill. We saw four herds of deer, two of them close to us. It was a beautiful sight.

Meanwhile I saw the sun sinking gradually, and I got quite alarmed lest we should be benighted, and we called anxiously for Sandy, who had gone away for a moment, to give a signal to come back. We then began our descent, "squinting" the hill, the ponies going as safely and securely as possible. As the sun went down the scenery became more and more beautiful, the sky crimson, golden-red and blue, and the hills looking purple and lilac, most exquisite, till at length it set, and the hues grew softer in the sky and the outlines of the hills sharper. I never saw anything so fine. It soon, however, grew very dark.

At length Albert met us, and he told me he had waited all the time for us, as he knew how anxious I should be. He had been very unlucky, and had lost his sport, for the rifle would not go off just when he could have shot some fine harts ; yet he was as merry and cheerful as if nothing had happened to disappoint him. We got down quite safely to the bridge ; our ponies going most surely, though it was quite dusk when we were at the bottom of the hill. We walked to the *Marble Lodge*, and then got into the pony carriage and drove home by very bright moonlight, which made everything look very lovely ; but the road made one a little nervous.

We saw a flight of ptarmigan, with their white wings, on the top of *Sron a Chro*, also plovers, grouse, and pheasants. We were safely home by a quarter to eight.

Tuesday, October 1.

At a quarter-past eight o'clock we started, and were very very sorry to leave *Blair* and the dear *Highlands !* Every little trifle and every spot I had become attached to; our life of quiet and liberty, everything was so pleasant, and all the Highlanders and people who went with us I had got to like so much. Oh! the dear hills, it made me very sad to leave them behind !

Lord Glenlyon rode with us, and we went back exactly the same road we came ; through *Killiecrankie, Pitlochrie,* saw *Logierait,* &c. The battle of *Killiecrankie* was fought in a field to your left, as you come from *Blair* and before you come to the pass ; and Lord Dundee was shot in a garden immediately above the field at *Urrard* (formerly called *Kinrory*) which belongs to Mr. Stewart of *Urrard ;* the Stewarts of *Urrard* used formerly to live on *Craig Urrard.* We reached *Dunkeld* at half-past eleven. Mr. Oswald and Mr. Patrick Small Keir, with a detachment of Highlanders, were there. We drove up to the door of the cottage at *Dunkeld* and got out there. It is beautifully situated and the cottage is very pretty, with a good view of the river from the windows. *Craig-y-Barns* is a fine rocky hill to the left as you drive from *Blair.*

We walked to look at the beginning of the new house which the late Duke of Athole commenced, but which has been left unfinished, and also at a beautiful larch-tree, the first that was brought to *Scotland.* I rode back on " Arghait Bhean "* for the last time, and took a sad leave of him and of faithful Sandy Mc Ara. We walked into the ruins of the old cathedral and into that part which the late Duke fitted up for service, and where there is a fine monument of him. I should never have recognized the grounds of *Dunkeld,* so different did they look without the encampment.† Beautiful as *Dunkeld* is, it does not approach the beauty and wildness of *Blair.*

After twelve o'clock we set off again, and to our astonishment Lord Glenlyon insisted upon riding on with us to *Dundee,* which is 50 miles from *Blair !* Captain J. Murray also rode with

* This pony was given to me by the Duke of Athole in 1847, and is now alive at Osborne.

† *Vide* page 21.

us from *Dunkeld.* It made me feel sad to see the country becoming flatter and flatter. There was a great crowd at *Cupar Angus,* and at *Dundee* a still larger one, and on the pier the crush was very great.

We took leave of Lord Glenlyon with real regret, and he seemed quite unhappy at our going. No one could be more zealous or kinder than he was.

There was a fearful swell when we went in the barge to the yacht.

Thursday, October 3.

The English coast appeared terribly flat. Lord Aberdeen was quite touched when I told him I was so attached to the dear, dear *Highlands* and missed the fine hills so much. There is a great peculiarity about the *Highlands* and Highlanders ; and they are such a chivalrous, fine, active people. Our stay among them was so delightful. Independently of the beautiful scenery, there was a quiet, a retirement, a wildness, a liberty, and a solitude that had such a charm for us.

The day had cleared up and was bright, but

the air very heavy and thick, quite different from the mountain air, which was so pure, light, and brisk. At two o'clock we reached *Woolwich*, and shortly after disembarked. We proceeded straight to the railroad, and arrived at *Windsor Castle* at a few minutes past four.

Tour round the West Coast of Scotland, and Visit to Ardverikie.

Wednesday, August 11, 1847.

We proceeded from the *Osborne Pier* on board the yacht. Our two eldest children, my brother Charles, the Duke and Duchess of Norfolk, Lord Grey (Secretary of State), Lady Jocelyn, General Wemyss, Sir James Clark, and Miss Hildyard, accompanied us.

We have with us the following steamers :— The "Black Eagle," "Garland," "Undine," "Fairy," and "Scourge" (war-steamers). The two equerries are on board the "Black Eagle."

We were soon under weigh, and as *Osborne* vanished from our sight, I thought of our poor children left behind.

On Board the Victoria and Albert,
in Dartmouth Harbour,
Thursday, August 12.

I have not much to relate. Our voyage has not been what we intended, *mais l'homme propose et Dieu dispose;* for instead of being at *Falmouth* we are only at *Dartmouth!* We started at five o'clock, and soon after felt the vessel stop, and on inquiring, heard that the fog was so thick it was impossible to proceed. At last Captain Smithett was sent out in the "Garland" to report on the state of the weather; and he soon returned, saying that all was clear enough to proceed outside *The Needles* (we were in *Alum Bay*). So we started again, and, after breakfast, we came on deck, where I remained working and talking; feeling quite well; but towards one the ground swell had increased, and we decided to run into the harbour we now are in.

On Board the Victoria and Albert,
Milford Haven, South Wales,
Saturday, August. 14.

Arrived here this afternoon at five. I will give an account of what has passed since leaving · *Dartmouth.* Thursday evening, after dining with Charles, we went on deck, and found the whole town illuminated, and the effect of its curious high houses running down quite into the still sea, which reflected the illumination, was lovely,—the night being so fine and calm.

Friday, August 13.

We started af four and reached the *Scilly Islands* at three in the afternoon; it had been very

rough. The numerous little rocky islands, in the midst of which we are lying, are very curious.

St. Mary's, the principal island, has a little

town, a church, and a small harbour. Exactly opposite, on the isle of *Tresco*, is Mr. Smith's house; he has the lease of all the islands from the Duchy of Cornwall. Farther to the left is *St. Agnes*, with a lighthouse and innumerable rocks.

Albert (who, as well as Charles, has not been unwell, while I suffered very much) went with Charles and Bertie to see one of the islands. The children recover from their sea-sickness directly. When Albert and the others returned, soon after five, we went with our ladies and gentlemen in the barge across the harbour,— where, blue as the sea was, it was still rather rough,—and landed at a little pier at *St. Mary's*. The harbour, surmounted by the old fort of the *Star Castle*, reminded me of the harbour of *St. Heliers*. We got into a pony carriage belonging to Mr. Smith, with Charles and Lady Jocelyn, and drove through the place, which looks like a small fishing town, and then round the fortifications of the castle, where there is a very pretty walk overhanging the sea; the rock being covered with fern, and heath, and furze. The extensive view of the islands and rocks around is very beautiful. The town is built upon a very narrow strip of land,

with a small bay on either side. We got out
at the old castle, which bears the date of one
of the Edwards. The view from the battlements
is very fine. We returned the same way we went,
a little before seven.

Saturday, August 14.

We started at five o'clock, and the yacht then
began to roll and pitch dreadfully, and I felt again
very unwell; but I came on deck at three in the
afternoon, the sea then was like glass, and we
were close to the Welsh coast.

This harbour, *Milford Haven*, is magnificent;
the largest we have; a fleet might lie here.
We are anchored just off *Mil-
ford. Pembroke* in front, in the
distance. The cliffs, which are
reddish brown, are not very
high. Albert and Charles went
in the "Fairy" to *Pembroke*,
and I sketched. Numbers of
boats came out, with Welsh-
women in their curious high-crowned men's hats;
and Bertie was much cheered, for the people seemed

greatly pleased to see the " Prince of Wales."
Albert returned at a quarter to eight.

A very pretty dairymaid, in complete Welsh
costume, was brought on board for me to see.
We found *Milford* illuminated when we went on
deck, and bonfires burning everywhere.

Sunday, August 15.

We started again at four o'clock, but this time
had a beautiful day, with the sea smooth the
whole way. About eleven we saw the moun-
tainous coast of *Caernarvonshire;* the hills, which
are in fact high mountains, are bold and finely
shaped, and, Albert said, reminded him much
of *Ischia*, with the beautiful deep blue sea and
bright sky.

Having arrived at the entrance of the *Menai
Straits*, we all left the " Victoria and Albert," and
went on board the " Fairy." The " Victoria and
Albert" with the " Black Eagle" (the two equerries
having joined us), the " Undine " and " Scourge,"
proceeded round the *Isle of Anglesea* by *Holy-
head*, and, in the " Fairy," accompanied by the

"Garland," we went into the *Straits.* As we entered, the view of the fine mountains with their rich verdure—*Snowdon* rising splendidly in the midst—and of the fields and woods below, was really glorious. To the left the country is extremely flat. Then *Caernarvon* came in sight, with its grand old Castle so finely situated. We stopped for a few moments off here, but did not land. The mountains disappeared for a while, and then re-appeared more beautiful than ever. We passed close to *Plas Newydd,* where we had spent six 'weeks fifteen years ago. I felt as if I remembered it all very well; but admired the scenery even more than I had expected from my previous recollection.

We passed the famous *Swilly Rocks,* and saw the works they are making for the tube for the railroad, and then went under the *Menai Bridge,* and stopped immediately on the other side. There were crowds of loyal people in steamers and boats, playing "God save the Queen," and cheering tremendously. Albert and Charles landed and walked over the bridge. When they returned we went on again, and stopped in a most beautiful spot, with almost Swiss scenery, opposite *Penrhyn*

Castle, Colonel Douglas Pennant's (which I saw in the late possessor's time unfinished), and near *Bangor,* with its wooded banks, through which one can see the high-road to *Beaumaris.* The purple hills, with the verdure below, and the blue sea, were extremely picturesque.

Albert and Charles went to see *Penrhyn.* As soon as they returned we dined below in the " Fairy," and at eight we returned, with the children and all our people, to the " Victoria and Albert." The evening was beautiful and the day very successful.

Monday, August 16.

We woke soon after four o'clock, when getting under weigh, and were surprised to feel the yacht stop not an hour after. Something had gone wrong with the paddle-wheel—just as happened last year—and it took full two hours to set it right. Then at seven we started afresh. A beautiful morning with a very smooth sea. By half-past ten we were in sight of the *Isle of Man,* which is a fine island with bold hills and cliffs. A little before twelve we reached the point of the bay, on which is the town of *Douglas*, very prettily situated, with a picturesque castle near the light-house, on the extreme point of the bay. We stopped off here for ten minutes or a quarter of an hour,—the rocks were covered with people. From *Douglas* to *Ramsay Bay* the hills and cliffs are high and bold ; though *Ramsay* itself is low.

For about two hours we were out of sight of land, and I was below writing. When I came on deck at three o'clock the Scotch coast was quite close ; the *Mull of Galloway*, and then *Wigtown-shire*. Albert declared he saw the Irish coast, but I could not descry it. At five we came in sight of *Loch Ryan*, and saw, to the left, *Ailsa Craig* rising more than 1,000 feet perpendicularly from the sea. *Loch Ryan* is very fine, and the hills and glens are lovely, particularly little *Glen Finnie*. The loch is very large, and the hills here are very high and wooded. The little town is called *Stranraer*.

Tuesday, August 17.

At six o'clock we began to move. A beautiful morning. At about eight we were close to the *Ailsa Rock* or *Craig*, the formation of which is very curious. There were thousands and thousands of birds,—gannets,—on the rock, and we fired a gun off three times in order to bring them in reach of a shot—Albert and Charles tried, but in vain. We next came in sight of the beautiful *Isle of Arran*. The finest point is when you are before the *Holy Island*, and in sight of the *Goatfell* range of mountains. The highest is about 2,800 feet; they are peculiarly fine from their bold pointed outlines. Before them is *Lamlash*. After passing *Holy Island* we came to *Brodick Bay*, which is beautiful, with high hills and a glen; in front of which, and surrounded by wood, is the castle which Lord Douglas is building. Not long after this we came in sight of the *Isle of Bute*, and entered the *Clyde*, the view of which from Mr. Stuart's and Lord Bute's property is beautiful : high wooded banks, the river opening out and widening, surrounded by the distant mountains. A small place to the right called *Largs* is very prettily situated.

At half-past twelve we reached *Greenock*, the port of *Glasgow*. The shore and the ships were crowded with people, there being no less (as I since learnt) than thirty-nine steamers, over-filled with people, which almost all followed us! Such a thing never was seen. Add to these steamers boats and ships of all descriptions, moving in all directions ; but not getting out of the way! We, however, got safe on board the "Fairy," and steamed up the *Clyde ;* it was hazy, and we could not see the distance well. We passed the small town of *Port Glasgow*, and about one o'clock were at *Dumbarton Castle.* Its situation is very fine, the rock rising straight out of the river, the mountains all round, and the town of *Dumbarton* behind it, making it very picturesque. We landed just below the Castle, and went with Charles and the children in a carriage to the fort. There was a great crowd, but excellent order kept. We went to the battery, but had to mount many steps to get to it. Wallace was confined here ; and it was one of the last castles which held out for Mary Queen of Scots. From the battery there is a very extensive view of the *Clyde* and *Dumbarton*, and we ought to have been able to see *Ben Lomond;* but it was in mist.

We got back to the "Fairy" by half-past two, and returned to *Greenock*, escorted by nineteen steamers. Steamed past *Greenock*, and went on towards *Loch Long*, passing *Roseneath* to the right, where the present Duke and Duchess of Argyll live. *Loch Long* is indeed splendid, 15 miles in length, surrounded by grand hills, with such beautiful outlines, and very green—all so different from the eastern part of *Scotland*—the loch winding along most beautifully, so as to seem closed at times. Charles said it reminded him of *Switzerland* and the *Tyrol*. The finest point of *Loch Long* is looking towards *Loch Goil.* We had a very good sight of the mountain called *The Cobbler;* the top of which resembles a man sitting and mending his shoe! At the end of the loch we got a glimpse of *Ben Lomond*, and were, in fact, very near *Loch Lomond.*

We returned as we came. There was no sun, and once or twice a little mist; but still it was beautiful. We went on to *Rothsay*, which we reached at eight o'clock, and immediately went on board the " Victoria and Albert," greatly tired but much amused and interested.

The children enjoy everything extremely, and bear the novelty and excitement wonderfully. The people cheered the " Duke of Rothsay " * very much, and also called for a cheer for the " Princess of Great Britain." Everywhere the good Highlanders are very enthusiastic. *Rothsay* is a pretty little town, built round a fine bay, with hills in the distance, and a fine harbour. When we went on deck after dinner, we found the whole town brilliantly illuminated, with every window lit up, which had a very pretty effect.

Wednesday, August 18.

A bright fresh morning, the hills slightly tipped with clouds. At eight o'clock we all went on board the " Fairy," and went up the *Kyles of Bute*, which, as you advance, become very fine, the

---

* A title belonging to the eldest son of the Sovereign of Scotland, and therefore held by the Prince of Wales as eldest son of the Queen, the representative of the ancient Kings of Scotland.

hills lying so curiously one behind the other, sometimes apparently closing up all outlet.

We saw *Arran* to the left, looking very grand in the distance. We have been turning about a good deal since yesterday, for we went by *Arran* and *Holy Island*, and then left *Little* and *Great Cumbray* to our left, and went up to *Dumbarton* and back, and on to *Loch Long*, and then to *Rothsay*, leaving *Arran* to our left; then, after passing *Arran*, we entered *Loch Fyne*. I, however, had a headache, and was obliged to lie down below, and only came on deck again when we were within an hour of *Inverary;* where the lake widens, and the hills on either side are very green and undulating, but not very high.

The approach to *Inverary* is splendid; the loch

is very wide ; straight before you a fine range of mountains splendidly lit up,—green, pink, and lilac ; to the left, the little town of *Inverary ;* and above it, surrounded by pine woods, stands the Castle of *Inverary*, square, with turrets at the corners.

Our reception was in the true Highland fashion. The Duke and Duchess of Argyll (dear Lady Elizabeth Leveson Gower), the Duchess of Sutherland, Lord Stafford, Lady Caroline Leveson Gower, and the Blantyres received us at the landing-place, which was all ornamented with heather. The Celtic Society, including Campbell of Islay, his two sons (one grown up and the other a very pretty little boy), with a number of his men, and several other Campbells, were all drawn up near to the carriage. We got into a carriage with the two Duchesses, Charles and the Duke being on the box (we had left the children on board the "Fairy"), and took a beautiful drive amongst magnificent trees, and along a glen where we saw *Ben Sheerar*, &c. The weather was particularly fine, and we were much struck by the extreme beauty of *Inverary*—presenting as it does such a combination of magnificent timber, with high mountains, and a noble lake.

The pipers walked before the carriage, and the Highlanders on either side, as we approached the house. Outside stood the Marquis of Lorn, just two years old, a dear, white, fat, fair little fellow with reddish hair, but very delicate features, like both his father and mother: he is such a merry, independent little child. He had a black velvet dress and jacket, with a " sporran," scarf, and Highland bonnet. We lunched at two with our hosts ; the Highland gentlemen standing with halberds in the room. We sent for our children, who arrived during luncheon time. We left *Inverary* before three, and took the children with us in the carriage. The Argylls, the Duchess of Sutherland, and the others, accompanied us on board the " Fairy," where we took leave of them.

The light on the hills was beautiful as we steamed down *Loch Fyne.* At five we reached *Lochgilp,* and all landed at *Lochgilphead,* a small village where there were numbers of people, and, amongst others, Sir John P. Orde, who lent his carriage and was extremely civil. We and our people drove through the little village to the *Crinan Canal,* where we entered a most magnificently decorated barge, drawn by three horses, ridden by postilions in scarlet. We glided along very smoothly, and the views of the hills—the range of *Cruachan*—were very fine indeed ; but the eleven locks we had to go through—(a very curious process, first passing several by rising, and then others by going down)—were tedious, and instead of the passage lasting one hour and a half, it lasted upwards of two hours and a half, therefore it was nearly eight o'clock before we reached *Loch Crinan.* We instantly went on board the " Victoria and Albert," but it was too late to proceed to *Oban ;* we had, therefore, to lengthen our voyage by a day, and spent the night at *Crinan.* It is a very fine spot, hills all round, and, in the distance, those of the island of *Jura.* The yacht had had a good passage round the *Mull of Cantire.* We dined with Charles, and went on deck ; and the blaze of the numerous bonfires—the half moon, the stars, and the extreme stillness of the night—had a charming effect.

Thursday, August 19.

A beautiful day. At nine o'clock we left *Crinan*, proceeding to the right, up splendid passes, with myriads of islands, and such enchanting views, that I cannot enumerate them. We passed first up the *Sound of Jura*, where numbers of people met us in small boats, decorated with little flags; then up the *Pass of Kerrera* to *Oban*, one of the finest spots we have seen, with the ruins of the old *Castle of Dunolly* and a range of high mountains in the distance. To the left, after leaving *Oban*, we saw the *Isle of Kerrera* and to the right *Dunstaffnage Castle*, whence came the famous stone which supports the " Coronation Chair," in which the sovereigns are crowned at *Westminster Abbey*. Alexander II. is said to be buried here. We passed close by the flat rock, called *The Lady's Rock*, on which a McLean left his wife, hoping she would be washed away—she was saved however.

We then came into the *Sound of Mull* by *Tobermory*, a small place prettily situated, and from thence the views continued beautiful. At

one o'clock we were in sight of the *Isles of Rum,
Eig* and *Muck* (rather large islands, which Lord
Salisbury bought a few years ago). Next we passed
the long, flat, curious islands of *Coll* and *Tiree*.
The inhabitants of these islands have, unhappily,
been terrible sufferers during the last winter
from famine. A little further on we saw, to our
right, the *Treshinish Isles*, very curiously-shaped
rocks : one is called *The Dutchman's Cap*, and
has the most strange shape, thus—

At three we anchored close before *Staffa*, and
immediately got into the barge with Charles, the
children, and the rest of our people, and rowed
towards the cave. As we rounded the point, the
wonderful basaltic formation came in sight. The
appearance it presents is most extraordinary ; and
when we turned the corner to go into the renowned
Fingal's Cave, the effect was splendid, like a great
entrance into a vaulted hall: it looked almost awful
as we entered, and the barge heaved up and down
on the swell of the sea. It is very high, but not

longer than 227 feet, and narrower than I expected, being only 40 feet wide. The sea is immensely deep in the cave. The rocks, under water, were all colours—pink, blue, and green—which had a most beautiful and varied effect. It was the first time the British standard with a Queen of Great Britain, and her husband and children, had ever entered *Fingal's Cave*, and the men gave three cheers, which sounded very impressive there. We backed out, and then went on a little further to look at the other cave, not of basaltic formation, and at the point called *The Herdsman*. The swell was beginning to get up, and perhaps an hour later we could not have gone in.

We returned to the yacht, but Albert and Charles landed again at *Staffa*. They returned in three quarters of an hour, and we then went on to *Iona;* here Albert and Charles landed, and were absent an hour. I and the ladies sketched. We saw from the yacht the ruins of the old cathedral of *St. Oran*. When Albert and Charles returned, they said the ruins were very curious, there had been two monasteries there, and fine old crosses and tombs of ancient kings were still to be seen. I must see it some other time. On Albert's return we went on again, and reached *Tobermory* at nine. The place was all illuminated.

Friday, August 20.

A wet morning when we rose at half-past seven, and it was pouring with rain when we left *Tobermory* at half-past eight. I went down, and drew and painted. It cleared up about half-past ten, and I came on deck. The scenery in *Loch Linnhe* was magnificent—such beautiful mountains. From *Loch Linnhe* we entered *Loch Eil*, and passed the entrance of *Loch Leven* to the right, at the end of which is *Glencoe*, so famous for its beautiful scenery and for the horrible massacre of the Macdonalds, in William III.'s time.

A little before one we arrived at *Fort William*, a very small place. The afternoon was very bright, and the scenery fine. After luncheon Albert and Charles set off in the " Fairy" to see *Glencoe*. They returned at twenty minutes past seven, and Albert thought *Glencoe* was very fine, though not quite as much so as he had expected. They had driven in an extraordinary carriage, with seats for thirty. The people, who recognized Albert, were so loyal that they took the horses out and insisted on drawing the carriage.

The evening was excessively cold and showery.

I am quite sorry we shall have to leave our yacht to-morrow, in which we have been so comfortably housed, and that this delightful voyage and tour among the Western Lochs and Isles is at an end—they are so beautiful,—and so full of poetry and romance, traditions, and historical associations.

Ardverikie, Loch Laggan,
Saturday, August 21.

Alas! a very wet morning. We were ready long before nine o'clock, but had to wait, as our carriages were not ready. At last we all landed at *Fort William,* where there was a great gathering of Highlanders, in their different tartans, with Lord Lovat and Mr. Stuart Mackenzie at their head. We got into our carriage with Charles and the two children; there was a great crowd to see us off. We went by a very wild and lonely road, the latter part extremely fine, with mountains and streams that reminded us of *Glen Tilt*. We changed horses only once, and came at length in sight of *Loch Laggan*. It is a beautiful lake (small in comparison to what we have seen) surrounded by very fine mountains : the road by its side is extremely pretty. We saw Lord Abercorn's house of *Ardverikie* long before we came to it. At *Laggan* there is only a small inn, and at the end of the lake, a ferry. Here, in spite of the pouring rain, were assembled a number of Highlanders, with Macpherson of Cluny (always called Cluny Macpherson) and three dear little boys of his, Davidson of Tulloch, and others, with Lord Abercorn, in full Highland dress. We stepped out of our carriage and stood upon the floating bridge, and so crossed over in two or three minutes. We then drove on, in our pony carriages, to *Ardverikie*, and arrived there in about · twenty minutes. It is quite close to the lake, and the view from the windows, as I now write, though obscured by rain, is very beautiful, and extremely wild. There is not a village, house, or cottage within four or five miles : one can only get to it by the ferry, or by rowing across the lake. The house is a comfortable shooting-lodge,

built of stone, with many nice rooms in it. Stags'
horns are placed along the outside and in the
passages ; and the walls of the drawing-room and
ante-room are ornamented with beautiful drawings
of stags, by Landseer.

There is little to say of our stay at *Ardverikie;*
the country is very fine, but the weather was most
dreadful.

On the 28th, about five o'clock, Albert drove
me out across the ferry, along the *Kingussie* road,
and from here the scenery was splendid : high
bold hills, with a good deal of wood ; glens, with
the *Pattock*, and a small waterfall ; the meadows
here and there, with people making hay, and
cottages sprinkled sparingly about, reminded us
much of *Thüringen.* We drove to the small
farm, where Colonel Macpherson now lives, called
Strathmashie, and back again, 16 miles in all.
We were delighted with the scenery, which is
singularly beautiful, wild and romantic,—with so
much fine wood about it, which greatly enhances
the beauty of a landscape.

Thursday, September 16.

Albert left at six this morning to go to *Inverness* and see the *Caledonian Canal.*

Friday, September 17.

At two o'clock I left *Ardverikie* with the children, and reached *Fort William* at half-past six, where I had the happiness of finding Albert on board the yacht. All had gone off well; but the weather had been very bad. Albert said *Dochfour* was beautiful; the house new and very elegant, with a fine garden, and Mr. and Lady Georgiana Baillie very pleasant people.

Albert had to go to *Inverness*, and to stay for a ball that was held there; and he was everywhere extremely well received. This morning he saw the *Falls of Foyers*, which, he tells me, are very grand indeed; and of a great height; and he says that the *Caledonian Canal* is a most remarkable work.

Loch Ryan,
Saturday, September 18.

At five o'clock we left *Fort William.* Rather a fine morning; but very squally, and the sea rough, even where we were. When we came on deck, we were close to the *Isle of Jura,* which has such a fine, bold outline. We went on to *Loch Crinan,* where we got into the barge : here it was very rough and pouring with rain, so unlike the beautiful evening when we were here a month ago. We landed at *Crinan.* Mr. Malcolm, whose castle is just opposite, received us there, and we entered the canal boat at ten. We proceeded more quickly than the last time ; the people kept running along as before, and there was a piper at each lock. It rained almost the whole time. We reached *Lochgilphead* at twelve, in pouring rain, and embarked on board the " Black Eagle." The yacht had again to go round the *Mull of Cantire* and meet us at *Campbeltown.* What a contrast to the weather we had when we came !

We got under weigh, and proceeded by

Kilbrannan Sound and *Arran.* We went on deck for a little while, but were driven below by the rain ; later, however, it was possible to keep on deck. We reached *Campbeltown,* a small and not pretty place, at the foot of *Cantire,* at twenty minutes to five. About half an hour after we arrived the yacht came in, with the " Garland," "Fairy," and " Scourge," and we immediately went on board. They had had a very bad passage, and Captain Crispin said he was very glad that we had not been on board the " Victoria and Albert." This rather alarmed us for the next day's voyage, the more so as the evening was squally and the sky very unpromising. There was a long consultation as to what was to be done, and at last it was decided that we should start at four in the morning, and if it were very rough, we should either run into *Loch Ryan,* the *Mull of Galloway,* the *Bay of Ramsay,* or into *Douglas* in the *Isle of Man.*

Loch Ryan,
Sunday, September 19.

We set off at four o'clock, the yacht rolling considerably; but it was quite bearable; however, at seven they came to shut down the port-holes, expecting a heavy sea, and Lord Adolphus saw Albert, who had just got up, and said it would be very rough; upon which it was decided to put back a little way, and to go into *Loch Ryan;* we accordingly did so, and anchored there at half-past eight; — such a dreary rainy day — one could hardly recognize what was so fine when we were last in here.

Both now, and the time before when we were in *Loch Ryan,* Lord Orkney very civilly sent us game and all sorts of things.

At twelve o'clock Lord Adolphus read the short sea service. We then talked over our voyage, and what could be done;—the day was very wretched,—pouring with rain and blowing hard. It was at last decided to start again at three, and get this evening to the *Mull of Galloway,* which would only take us three hours, though it would probably be rough. As soon as we were out of the loch the yacht began to pitch, and the sea was dreadfully rough. I was very ill. Albert, however, stood it perfectly, and the children very tolerably. Presently we came in sight of the *Mull of Galloway*, a great rock with a lighthouse on it ;—and this was our last glimpse of dear *Scotland*.

Monday, September 20.

At six o'clock we got under weigh, and after considerable " rockings," which lasted for nearly two hours, we were near the *Isle of Man*, in smooth water, and at half-past eight anchored in *Ramsay Bay*.

Albert went on shore, and meantime the Bishop of Sodor and Man, with others, came on board. Albert returned at twelve. At one o'clock we started again. We had to go slowly at first, as our paddle-wheel again got wrong, and because we should otherwise have arrived before we were expected.

We anchored at seven in *Fleetwood Harbour ;*

the entrance was extremely narrow and difficult. We were lashed close to the pier, to prevent our being turned by the tide; and when I went on deck there was a great commotion, such running and calling, and pulling of ropes, &c. It was a cheerless evening, blowing hard.

Tuesday, September 21.

At ten o'clock we landed, and proceeded by rail to *London.*

LIFE IN THE HIGHLANDS,

1848 TO 1861.

Land of brown heath and shaggy wood,
Land of the mountain and the flood,
Land of my sires! what mortal hand
Can e'er untie the filial band
That knits me to thy rugged strand!
Still, as I view each well-known scene,
Think what is now, and what hath been,
Seems as, to me, of all bereft,
Sole friends thy woods and streams are left;
And thus I love them better still,
Even in extremity of ill.

The Lay of the Last Minstrel.

First Impressions of Balmoral.

———

Balmoral,
Friday, September 8, 1848.

We arrived at *Balmoral* at a quarter to three. It is a pretty little castle in the old Scottish style. There is a picturesque tower and garden in front, with a high wooded hill; at the back there is wood down to the *Dee;* and the hills rise all around.

There is a nice little hall, with a billiard-room; next to it is the dining-room. Upstairs (ascending by a good broad staircase) immediately to the right, and above the dining-room, is our sitting-room (formerly the drawing-room), a fine large room—next to which is our bed-room, opening into a little dressing-room which is Albert's. Opposite, down a few steps, are the children's and Miss Hildyard's three rooms. The ladies live below, and the gentlemen upstairs.

We lunched almost immediately, and at half-

past four we walked out, and went up to the top
of the wooded hill opposite our windows, where
there is a cairn, and up which there is a pretty
winding path. The view from here, looking
down upon the house, is charming. To the left
you look towards the beautiful hills surrounding
Loch-na-Gar, and to the right, towards *Ballater*,
to the glen (or valley) along which the *Dee* winds,
with beautiful wooded hills, which reminded us very
much of the *Thüringerwald*. It was so calm, and
so solitary, it did one good as one gazed around ;
and the pure mountain air was most refreshing.
All seemed to breathe freedom and peace, and to
make one forget the world and its sad turmoils.

The scenery is wild, and yet not desolate ; and
everything looks much more prosperous and cultivated than at *Laggan*. Then the soil is delightfully dry. We walked beside the *Dee*, a beautiful,
rapid stream, which is close behind the house.
The view of the hills towards *Invercauld* is
exceedingly fine.

When I came in at half-past six, Albert went out
to try his luck with some stags which lay quite close
in the woods, but he was unsuccessful. They
come down of an evening quite near to the house.

First Ascent of Loch-na-Gar.

Saturday, September 16, 1848.

At half-past nine o'clock Albert and I set off in a postchaise, and drove to the bridge in the wood of *Balloch Buie*, about five miles from *Balmoral*, where our ponies and people were. Here we mounted, and were attended by a keeper of Mr. Farquharson's as guide, Macdonald*—who, with his shooting-jacket, and in his kilt, looked a picture—Grant† on a pony, with our luncheon in two

---

* A Jäger of the Prince's, who came from Fort Augustus in the west: he was remarkably tall and handsome. The poor man died of consumption at Windsor, in May, 1860. His eldest son was Attaché to the British Legation in Japan. He died in 1866. The third son, Archie, is Jäger to the Prince of Wales, and was for a year with the beloved Prince.

† Head-keeper. He had been nearly twenty years with Sir Robert Gordon, nine as keeper; he was born in Braemar, in the year 1810. He is an excellent man, most trustworthy, of singular shrewdness and discretion, and most devotedly attached to the Prince and myself. He has a fine intelligent

baskets, and Batterbury* on another pony. We went through that beautiful wood for about a mile, and then turned and began to ascend gradually, the view getting finer and finer; no road, but not bad ground — moss, heather, and stones. Albert saw some deer when we had been out about three-quarters of an hour, and ran off to stalk them, while I rested; but he arrived just a minute too late. He waited for me on the other side of a stony little burn, which I crossed on my pony, after our faithful Highlanders had moved some stones and made it easier. We then went on a little way, and I got off and walked a bit, and afterwards remounted; Macdonald leading my pony. The view of *Ben-na-Bhourd*, and indeed of all around, was very beautiful; but as

countenance. The Prince was very fond of him. He has six sons,—the second, Alick, is wardrobe-man to our son Leopold: all are good, well-disposed lads, and getting on well in their different occupations. His mother, a fine, hale, old woman of eighty years, "stops" in a small cottage which the Prince built for her in our village. He, himself, lives in a pretty Lodge called Croft, a mile from Balmoral, which the Prince built for him.

* A groom (now dead some years) who followed me in his ordinary dress, with thin boots and gaiters, and seemed anything but happy. He hardly ever attended me after this.

we rose higher we saw mist over *Loch-na-Gar*.
Albert left me to go after ptarmigan, and went on
with Grant, while the others remained with me,
taking the greatest care of me. Macdonald is a
good honest man, and was indefatigable, and poor
Batterbury was very anxious also.

I saw ptarmigan get up, and Albert fire—he
then disappeared from my sight, and I rode on.
It became cold and misty when we were on *Loch-na-Gar*. In half an hour, or rather less, Albert
rejoined me with two ptarmigan, having come up
by a shorter way. Here it was quite soft, easy
walking, and we looked down on two small
lochs called *Na Nian*, which were very striking,
being so high up in the hills. Albert was
tired, and remounted his pony; I had also been
walking a little way. The ascent commenced,
and with it a very thick fog, and when we
had nearly reached the top of *Loch-na-Gar*,
the mist drifted in thick clouds so as to hide
everything not within one hundred yards of us.
Near the peak (the fine point of the mountain which is seen so well from above Grant's
house) we got off and walked, and climbed up
some steep stones, to a place where we found a

seat in a little nook, and had some luncheon. It
was just two o'clock, so we had taken four hours
going up.

But, alas! nothing whatever to be seen; and it
was cold, and wet, and cheerless. At about twenty
minutes after two we set off on our way down-
wards, the wind blowing a hurricane, and the mist
being like rain, and everything quite dark with it.
Bowman (Mr. Farquharson's keeper) and Macdonald, who preceded us, looked like ghosts. We
walked some way till I was quite breathless, and
remounted my pony, well wrapped up in plaids;
and we came down by the same path that Albert
had come up, which is shorter, but steeper; the
pony went delightfully; but the mist made me
feel cheerless.

Albert kept ahead a little while for ptarmigan,
but he gave it up again. When we had gone on
about an hour and a quarter, or an hour and a
half, the fog disappeared like magic, and all was
sunshine below, about one thousand feet from the
top I should say. Most provoking!—and yet one
felt happy to see sunshine and daylight again.

The view, as one descends, overlooking *Invercauld* and the wood which is called *Balloch Buie*,

is most lovely. We saw some deer in the wood below. We rode on till after we passed the burn, and had nearly got to the wood. We came another way down, by a much rougher path; and then, from the road in the wood, we walked up to the *Falls of the Garbhalt*, which are beautiful. The rocks are very grand, and the view from the little bridge, and also from a seat a little lower down, is extremely pretty. We found our carriages in the road, and drove home by six o'clock.

We met Captain Gordon, and then Lord John Russell and Sir James Clark. They had come to look after us, and when we got home we found the two ladies at the door waiting most anxiously for us.

A " DRIVE " IN THE BALLOCH BUIE.

September 18, 1848.

At a quarter-past ten o'clock we set off in a postchaise with Bertie, and drove beyond the house of Mr. Farquharson's keeper in the *Balloch Buie*. We then mounted our ponies, Bertie riding Grant's pony on the deer-saddle, and being led by a gillie, Grant walking by his side. Macdonald and several gillies were with us, and we were preceded by Bowman and old Arthur Farquharson, a deer-stalker of Invercauld's. They took us up a beautiful path winding through the trees and heather in the *Balloch Buie;* but when we had got about a mile or more they discovered deer. A " council of war " was held in a whisper, and we turned back and went the whole way down again, and rode along to the keeper's lodge, where we turned up the glen immediately below *Craig Daign*, through a beautiful part of the

wood, and went on along the track, till we came
to the foot of the craig, where we all dismounted.

We scrambled up an almost perpendicular place
to where there was a little *box*, made of hurdles
and interwoven with branches of fir and heather,
about five feet in height. There we seated ourselves with Bertie, Macdonald lying in the heather
near us, watching and quite concealed; some had
gone round to beat, and others again were at a
little distance. We sat quite still, and sketched
a little; I doing the landscape and some trees,
Albert drawing Macdonald as he lay there.
This lasted for nearly an hour, when Albert
fancied he heard a distant sound, and, in a few
minutes, Macdonald whispered that he saw stags,
and that Albert should wait and take a steady
aim. We then heard them coming past. Albert
did not look over the box, but through it, and
fired through the branches, and then again over
the box. The deer retreated; but Albert felt
certain he had hit a stag. He ran up to the
keepers, and at that moment they called from
below that they " had got him," and Albert ran
on to see. I waited for a bit; but soon scrambled
on with Bertie and Macdonald's help; and Albert

joined me directly, and we all went down and saw
a magnificent stag, "a royal," which had dropped,
soon after Albert had hit him, at one of the men's
feet. The sport was successful, and every one
was delighted,—Macdonald and the keepers in
particular ;—the former saying, "that it was her
Majesty's coming out that had brought the good
luck." I was supposed to have "a lucky foot,"
of which the Highlanders "think a great deal."
We walked down to the place we last came up,
got into the carriage, and were home by half-past
two o'clock.

THE FIRST STAY AT ALT-NA-GIUTHASACH.

August 30, 1849.

After writing our letters, we set off on our ponies, with Miss Dawson,* Macdonald, Grant, Batterbury, and Hamis Coutts; Hamis is Gaelic for James, and is pronounced " Hamish." The road has been improved since last year, and though it is still very rough, there are no fords to pass, nor real difficulties any longer. We rode the whole way, and Albert only walked the last two miles. He took a Gaelic lesson during our ride, asking Macdonald, who speaks it with great purity, many words, and making him talk to Jemmie Coutts. Albert has already picked up many words : but it is a very difficult language, for it is pronounced in a totally different way from that in which it is written.

We arrived at our little " bothie " at two o'clock, and were amazed at the transformation. There are two huts, and to the one in which we

* Now Hon. Mrs. Parnell.

live a wooden addition has been made. We have a charming little dining-room, sitting-room, bed-room, and dressing-room, all *en suite;* and there is a little room where Caroline Dawson (the Maid of Honour) sleeps, one for her maid, and a little pantry. In the other house, which is only a few yards distant, is the kitchen, where the people generally sit, a small room where the servants dine, and another, which is a sort of store-room, and a loft above in which the men sleep. Margaret French (my maid), Caroline's maid, Löhlein * (Albert's valet), a cook, Shackle† (a footman), and Macdonald, are the only people with us in the house, old John Gordon and his wife excepted. Our rooms are delightfully papered, the ceilings as well as walls, and very nicely furnished. We lunched as soon as we arrived, and at three walked down (about twenty minutes'

---

* This faithful and trusty valet nursed his dear master most devotedly through his sad illness in December, 1861, and is now always with me as my personal groom of the chambers or valet. I gave him a house near Windsor Castle, where he resides when the Court are there. He is a native of Coburg. His father has been for fifty years Förster at Fülbach, close to Coburg.

† Who was very active and efficient. He is now a Page.

walk) to the loch called " Muich ; " which some say means "darkness" or " sorrow." Here we found a large boat, into which we all got, and Macdonald, Duncan, Grant, and Coutts rowed; old John Gordon and two others going in another boat with the net. They rowed up to the head of the loch, to where the *Muich* runs down out of the *Dhu Loch*, which is on the other side.

The scenery is beautiful here, so wild and grand, —real severe Highland scenery, with trees in the hollow. We had various scrambles in and out of the boat and along the shore, and saw three hawks, and caught seventy trout. I wish an artist could have been there to sketch the scene; it was so picturesque—the boat, the net, and the people in their kilts in the water, and on the shore. In going back, Albert rowed and Macdonald steered ; and the lights were beautiful.

We came home at a quarter-past seven. At eight we dined. Löhlein, Macdonald, and Shackle waiting on us. After dinner we played with Caroline Dawson at whist with dummy, and afterwards walked round the little garden. The silence and solitude, only interrupted by the waving of the fir-trees, were very solemn and striking.

A Beat in the Abergeldie Woods.

———

September 3, 1849.

At a quarter-past eleven we drove (the three gentlemen going in another carriage) to the road along which we went with Lord Portman the other day, and up to a small path, where I mounted my pony, Albert and the others walking. We came to *Geannachoil*, and Albert was much pleased with the splendid view. The lights were most beautiful, but the heat was overpowering, and the sun burning.

We turned to the right when out on the moors, where I got off and walked; and we seated ourselves behind a large stone, no one but Macdonald with us, who loaded the guns, and gave notice when anything was to be seen, as he lay upon the ground. The gentlemen were below in the road; the wood was beat, but nothing came, so we walked on and came down a beautiful thickly-wooded glen; and after a good deal of scrambling to get there, and to get up one side of the glen, we sat down again. We then scrambled over to the opposite side, where we again concealed ourselves ; in this beat Albert shot a roe, and I think would have shot more had they not been turned back by the sudden appearance of an old woman who, looking like a witch, came along through the wood with two immense crutches, and disturbed the whole thing. Albert killed the roe just as she was coming along, and the shot startled her very much ; she was told to come down, which she did, and sat below in the glen, motionless, having covered her head with her handkerchief. When two of the beaters came down and were told to take up the roe, they first saw the old woman, and started, and stared with horror—which was very amusing to see. I rode a little way afterwards, and then we seated ourselves behind a bush, in the rear of the wood, close to the distillery ; but this beat brought nothing. Albert killed a young black cock before we came to the second beat. We were home at a quarter-past three o'clock.

Visit to the Dhu Loch, &c.

September 11, 1849.

The morning was very fine. I heard the children repeat some poetry in German, and then at ten o'clock we set off with Lady Douro * in our carriage, and drove on beyond *Inch Bobbard*, changing horses near *Birkhall*, and stopping for a moment at the *Linn of Muich ;* here we found the ponies, which we mounted, forded the river, and were almost immediately at the hut. We stopped there only for an instant, and remounted our ponies directly; Grant, Macdonald (who led my pony the whole time, and was extremely useful and attentive), Jemmie Coutts (leading Lady Douro's pony), Charlie Coutts, and John Brown going with us : old John Gordon leading the way. It was half-past twelve when we began ascending the hill immediately behind the house, and pro-

* Now Duchess of Wellington.

ceeded along over the hills, to a great height, whence the view was very fine, quite overhanging the loch, and commanding an extensive view of *Glen Muich* beyond on the opposite side. The road got worse and worse. It was particularly bad when we had to pass the *Burn of the Glassalt*, which falls into the loch, and was very full. There had been so much rain, that the burns and rivers were very full, and the ground quite soft. We rode over the *Strone Hill*, the wind blowing dreadfully hard when we came to the top. Albert walked almost from the first, and shot a hare and a grouse; he put up a good many of them. We walked to a little hollow immediately above the *Dhu Loch*, and at half-past three seated ourselves there, and had some very welcome luncheon. The loch is only a mile in length, and very wild; the hills, which are very rocky and precipitous, rising perpendicularly from it.

In about half an hour we began our journey homewards. We came straight down beside the *Muich*, which falls in the most beautiful way over the rocks and stones in the glen. We rode down, and only had to get off to cross the *Glassalt*, which was an awkward ford to scramble over.

The road was rough, but certainly far less soft and disagreeable than the one we came by. I rode "Lochnagar" at first, but changed him for Colonel Gordon's pony, as I thought he took fright at the bogs; but Colonel Gordon's was broken-winded, and struggled very much in the soft ground, which was very disagreeable.

We were only an hour coming down to the boat. The evening was very fine, but it blew very hard on the lake and the men could not pull, and I got so alarmed that I begged to land, and Lady Douro was of my opinion that it was much better to get out. We accordingly landed, and rode home along a sort of sheep-path on the side of the lake, which took us three-quarters of an hour. It was very rough and very narrow, for the hill rises abruptly from the lake; we had seven hundred feet above us, and I suppose one hundred feet below. However, we arrived at the hut quite safely at twenty minutes to seven, thankful to have got through all our difficulties and adventures, which are always very pleasant to look back upon.

We dined a little before eight with Lady Douro, and played two rubbers of whist with her.

Old John Gordon amused Albert by saying, in speaking of the bad road we had gone, " It's something steep and something rough," and " this is the only best," meaning that it was *very* bad,—which was a characteristic reply.

.

ASCENT OF BEN-NA-BHOURD.

September 6, 1850.

At half-past ten o'clock we set off with Lady Douro and Ernest Leiningen,[*] and drove to *Invercauld*, about three-quarters of a mile beyond the house, where we found our people and ponies, together with Arthur Farquharson, Shewin, and others. We then walked a little way, after which we mounted our ponies and began the ascent towards *Ben-na-Bhourd;* Macdonald leading my pony, good little "Lochnagar," and James Coutts Lady Douro's. There is an excellent path, almost a narrow road, made up to within the last two miles and a half, which are very steep and rocky. The scenery is beautiful. We first rode up a glen (where a stone of the house in which Finla, the first of the Farquharsons, was born, is still shown,) through which the *Glassalt* runs. Further on comes a very narrow, rocky, and precipitous

[*] Our nephew.

glen, called the *Sluggan*, said to mean the
" swallow," or " swallowing." Some little distance
after this the country opens widely before you,
with *Ben-na-Bhourd* rising towards the left; and
then you enter the *Forest of Mar*, which the Duke
of Leeds rents from Lord Fife. There is a very
pretty little shooting-box, called *Sluggan Cottage*,
which is half way from *Invercauld* to the top
of *Ben-na-Bhourd.* Below this is the *Quoich*,
which we forded. The last bit of the real road is
a long steep ascent on the brow of a hill, the name
of which means the " Tooth's craig." (Macdonald
translated all the names for us.) The ascent, after
the path ceases, is very stony ; in fact, nothing but
bare granite. Albert had walked a great deal, and
we ladies got off after it became more uneven, and
when we were no longer very far from the top.
We came upon a number of " cairngorms," which
we all began picking up, and found some very
pretty ones. At the top, which is perfectly flat,
the ground is entirely composed of stones or wet
swampy moss, and the granite seems to have
stopped just a few feet below. We sat down at a
cairn, and had our luncheon. The wind was
extremely cold, but whenever we got out of it, the

air was very hot. The view from the top was magnificent and most extensive : *Ben-na-Bhourd* is 3,940 feet high. We saw *Ben-y-Ghlo* very clearly, *Cairngorm* and *Ben Muich Dhui* quite close but in another direction; the *Moray Firth*, and, through the glass, ships even could be seen ; and on the other side rose *Loch-na-Gar*, still the jewel of all the mountains here.

After luncheon we began our downward progress, and walked the whole of the steep part till we reached the path ; we came down very quickly, my pony making great haste, though he had half a mind to kick. Albert found some beautiful little rock crystals in the *Sluggan*, and walked the remainder of the way ; we ladies left our horses about a quarter of a mile before we met the carriage. The whole distance from *Invercauld* to the top of *Ben-na-Bhourd* is nine miles, so we must have been at least 18 miles riding and walking. It has been a delightful expedition. It was six o'clock when we reached the carriage, and we were home at a little past seven.

The Gathering.

September 12, 1850.

We lunched early, and then went at half-past two o'clock, with the children and all our party, except Lady Douro, to the Gathering at the *Castle of Braemar*, as we did last year. The Duffs, Far-quharsons, the Leeds's, and those staying with them, and Captain Forbes * and forty of his men who had come over from *Strath Don*, were there.† Some of our people were there also. There were the usual games of "putting the stone," "throwing the hammer" and "caber," and racing up the hill of *Craig Cheunnich*, which was accomplished in less than six minutes and a half; and we were all much pleased to see our gillie Duncan, ‡ who

* Now Sir Charles Forbes, of Castle Newe.

† A work shortly to be published, entitled *Highlanders of Scotland*, by Kenneth Macleay, Esq., R.S.A., contains excellent portraits of some of the men of these and other of the principal Highland clans, as well as of the Retainers of the Royal House-hold.

‡ One of our keepers since 1851 : an excellent, intelligent

is an active, good-looking, young man, win. He was far before the others the whole way. It is a fearful exertion. Mr. Farquharson brought him up to me afterwards. Eighteen or nineteen started, and it looked very pretty to see them run off in their different coloured kilts, with their white shirts (the jackets or doublets they take off for all the games), and scramble up through the wood, emerging gradually at the edge of it, and climbing the hill.

After this we went into the castle, and saw some dancing; the prettiest was a reel by Mr. Farquharson's children and some other children, and the " Ghillie Callum " beautifully danced by John Athole Farquharson, the fourth son. The twelve children were all there, including the baby, who is two years old.

Mama, Charles, and Ernest joined us at *Braemar*. Mama enjoys it all very much; it is her first visit to *Scotland*. We left after the dancing.

man, much liked by the Prince. He, like many others, spit blood after running the race up that steep hill in this short space of time, and he has never been so strong since. The running up hill has in consequence been discontinued. He lives in a cottage at the back of Craig Gowan (commanding a beautiful view) called Robrech, which the Prince built for him.

SALMON LEISTERING.

September 13, 1850.

We walked with Charles, the boys, and Vicky to the river side above the bridge, where all our tenants were assembled with poles and spears, or rather "leisters," for catching salmon. They all went into the river, walking up it, and then back again, poking about under all the stones to bring fish up to where the men stood with the net. It had a very pretty effect; about one hundred men wading through the river, some in kilts with poles and spears, all very much excited. Not succeeding the first time, we went higher up, and moved to three or four different places, but did not get any salmon; one or two escaping. Albert stood on a stone, and Colonel Gordon and Lord James Murray waded about the whole time. Duncan, in spite of all his exertions yesterday, and having besides walked to and from the Gathering, was the whole time in the water. Not far from the laundry there was another trial, and here we had a great fright. In one place there was a very deep pool, into which two men very foolishly went, and one could not swim; we suddenly saw them sink, and in one moment they seemed drowning, though surrounded by people. There was a cry for help, and a general rush, including Albert, towards the spot, which frightened me so much, that I grasped Lord Carlisle's arm in great agony. However, Dr. Robertson* swam in and pulled the man out, and all was safely over; but it was a horrid moment.

A salmon was speared here by one of the men; after which we walked to the ford, or quarry, where we were very successful, seven salmon being caught, some in the net, and some speared. Though Albert stood in the water some time he caught nothing: but the scene at this beautiful spot was exciting and picturesque in the extreme. I wished for Landseer's pencil. The sun was intensely hot. We did not get back till after three

---

* The gentleman who has had from the beginning the entire management of our property at Balmoral, &c. He is highly esteemed, and is a most amiable man, who has carried out all the Prince's and my wishes admirably.

o'clock, and then took luncheon. The Duchess of Gordon came to see us afterwards; and while she was still with us, Captain Forbes (who had asked permission to do so) marched through the grounds with his men, the pipers going in front. They stopped, and cheered three-times-three, throwing up their bonnets. They then marched off; and we listened with pleasure to the distant shouts and the sound of the pibroch.

We heard afterwards that our men had carried all Captain Forbes's men on their backs through the river. They saw the fishing going on, and came to the water's edge on the opposite side; and on being greeted by our people, said they would come over, on which ours went across in one moment and carried them over—Macdonald at their head carrying Captain Forbes on his back. This was very courteous, and worthy of chivalrous times.

LOCH MUICH.

September 16, 1850.

We reached the hut at three o'clock. At half-past four we walked down to the loch, and got into the boat with our people : Duncan, J. Brown,*

* The same who, in 1858, became my regular attendant out of doors everywhere in the Highlands ; who commenced as gillie in 1849, and was selected by Albert and me to go with my carriage. In 1851 he entered our service permanently, and began in that year leading my pony, and advanced step by step by his good conduct and intelligence. His attention, care, and faithfulness cannot be exceeded ; and the state of my health, which of late years has been sorely tried and weakened, renders such qualifications most valuable, and indeed, most needful in a constant attendant upon all occasions. He has since (in December, 1865), most deservedly, been promoted to be an upper servant, and my permanent personal attendant. He has all the independence and elevated feelings peculiar to the Highland race, and is singularly straightforward, simple-minded, kind-hearted, and disinterested; always ready to oblige ; and of a discretion rarely to be met with. He is now in his fortieth year. His father was a small farmer, who lived at the Bush on the opposite side to Balmoral. He is the second of

P. Coutts,* and Leys rowing. They rowed mostly towards the opposite side, which is very fine indeed, and deeply furrowed by the torrents, which form glens and corries where birch and alder trees grow close to the water's edge. We landed on a sandy spot below a fine glen, through which flows the *Black Burn*. It was very dry here; but still very picturesque, with alder-trees and mountain-ash in full fruit overhanging it. We afterwards landed at our usual place at the head of the loch, which is magnificent; and rode back. A new road has been made, and an excellent one it is, winding along above the lake.

The moon rose, and was beautifully reflected on the lake, which, with its steep green hills, looked lovely. To add to the beauty, poetry, and wildness of the scene, Coutts played in the boat; the men, who row very quickly and well now, giving an occasional shout when he played

nine brothers,—three of whom have died—two are in Australia and New Zealand, two are living in the neighbourhood of Balmoral; and the youngest, Archie (Archiebald) is valet to our son Leopold, and is an excellent, trustworthy young man.

* Now, since some years, piper to Farquharson of Invercauld.

a reel. It reminded me of Sir Walter Scott's
lines in *The Lady of the Lake*:—

> " Ever, as on they bore, more loud
> And louder rung the pibroch proud.
> At first the sound, by distance tame,
> Mellow'd along the waters came,
> And, lingering long by cape and bay,
> Wail'd every harsher note away."

We were home at a little past seven; and it was
so still and pretty as we entered the wood, and
saw the light flickering from our humble little
abode.

Torch-Light Ball at Corriemulzie.

———

September 10, 1852.

. We dined at a quarter-past six o'clock in morning gowns, (not ordinary ones, but such as are worn at a "breakfast,") and at seven started for *Corriemulzie,* for a *torch-light ball* in the open air. I wore a white bonnet, a grey watered silk, and (according to Highland fashion) my plaid scarf over my shoulder; and Albert his Highland dress which he wears every evening. We drove in the postchaise; the two ladies, Lord Derby and Colonel Gordon following in the other carriage.

It was a mild though threatening evening, but fortunately it kept fine. We arrived there at half-past eight, by which time, of course, it was quite dark. Mr. and Lady Agnes Duff * received us at the door, and then took us at once through the

* Now Earl and Countess of Fife.

house to the open space where the ball was, which was hid from our view till the curtains were drawn asunder. It was really a beautiful and most unusual sight. All the company were assembled there. A space about one hundred feet in length and sixty feet in width was boarded, and entirely surrounded by Highlanders bearing torches, which were placed in sockets, and constantly replenished. There were seven pipers, playing together, Mackay * leading—and they received us with the usual salute and three cheers, and "Nis! nis! nis!" (pronounced: "Neesh! "neesh! neesh!" the Highland "Hip! hip! hip!") and again cheers; after which came a most animated reel. There were above sixty people, exclusive of the Highlanders, of whom there were also sixty; all the Highland gentlemen, and any who were at all Scotch, were in kilts, the ladies in evening dresses. The company and the Highlanders danced pretty nearly alternately. There were two or three sword dances. We were upon

* My Piper from the year 1843, considered almost the first in Scotland, who was recommended by the Marquis of Breadalbane; he unfortunately went out of his mind in the year 1854, and died in 1855. A brother of his was Piper to the Duke of Sussex.

a *haut pas*, over which there was a canopy. The whole thing was admirably done, and very well worth seeing. Albert was delighted with it. I must not omit to mention a reel danced by eight Highlanders holding torches in their hands.

We left at half-past nine o'clock, and were home by a little past eleven. A long way certainly (14 miles I believe).

Account of the News of the Duke of Wellington's Death.

Alt-na-Giuthasach,
Thursday, September 16, 1852.

We were startled this morning, at seven o'clock, by a letter from Colonel Phipps, enclosing a telegraphic despatch with the report, from the sixth edition of the *Sun*, of the Duke of Wellington's death the day before yesterday, which report, however, we did not at all believe. Would to God that we had been right; and that this day had not been cruelly saddened in the afternoon.

We breakfasted with Miss Seymour ;* and, after writing and reading, we started at a quarter to eleven with her and our Highland party. The day was not cold, and would, in fact, have been very fine, if it had not been for a constant succession of very slight showers, or clouds coming down.

* Now Hon. Lady Biddulph.

We walked along the loch, the road up to which is excellent. It has been widened and would admit of a carriage. We arrived at the *Alt-na-Dearg*, a small burn and fall, which is very fine and rapid. Up this a winding path has been made, upon which we rode; though some parts are rather steep for riding. The burn falls over red granite; and in the ravine grow birch, mountain-ash, and alder. We got off and walked a good long way on the top of the very steep hills overhanging the loch, to the *Stron*, and the *Moss of Mon Elpie*, whence you overlook all the country belonging to Lord Panmure, *Mount Keen*, the *Ogilvie Hills*, &c. We stopped to rest a little while— though the walking is excellent, so hard and dry —on a point overlooking the *Shiel of the Glassalt*, and the head of the loch. Here I suddenly missed my watch, which the dear old Duke had given me; and, not being certain whether I had put it on or not, I asked Mackenzie * to go back and inquire. We walked on until we reached the higher part of the *Glassalt*, which we stepped across. We had passed over the tops of

* One of our keepers and a very good man; he lives at Alt-na-Giuthasach.

these hills on that expedition to the *Dhu Loch* three years ago, when the ground was so soft, that ponies could scarcely get along, the roads were so very bad.

Then we began the descent of the *Glassalt*, along which another path has been admirably made. From here it is quite beautiful, so wild and grand. The falls are equal to those of the *Bruar* at *Blair*, and are 150 feet in height; the whole height to the foot of the loch being 500 feet. It looked very picturesque to see the ponies and Highlanders winding along. We came down to the *Shiel of the Glassalt*, lately built, where there is a charming room for us, commanding a most lovely view. Here we took the cold luncheon, which we had brought with us; and after that we mounted our ponies, and rode to the *Dhu Loch*, along a beautiful path which keeps well above the burn, that rushes along over flat great slabs of stone. The scenery is exquisite. We passed a small fall called the *Burn of the Spullan* ("spout"). In half or three quarters of an hour we were at the wild and picturesque *Dhu Loch*.

We got off our ponies, and I had just sat down to sketch, when Mackenzie returned, saying

my watch was safe at home, and bringing letters :
amongst them there was one from Lord Derby,
which I tore open, and alas! it contained the
confirmation of the fatal news : that *England's*,
or rather *Britain's* pride, her glory, her hero, the
greatest man she ever had produced, was no
more! Sad day! Great and irreparable national
loss!

Lord Derby enclosed a few lines from Lord
Charles Wellesley, saying that his dear great
father had died on Tuesday at three o'clock, after
a few hours' illness and no suffering. God's
will be done! The day must have come: the
Duke was eighty-three. It is well for him that
he has been taken when still in the possession of
his great mind, and without a long illness,—but
what a *loss!* One cannot think of this country
without "the Duke,"—our immortal hero!

In him centered almost every earthly honour a
subject could possess. His position was the
highest a subject ever had,—above party,—looked
up to by all,—revered by the whole nation,—the
friend of the Sovereign ;—and *how* simply he
carried these honours! With what singleness
of purpose, what straightforwardness, what courage,

were all the motives of his actions guided. The
Crown never possessed,—and I fear never *will*—
so *devoted*, loyal, and faithful a subject, so staunch
a supporter! To *us* (who alas! have lost, now,
so many of our valued and experienced friends,)
his loss is *irreparable*, for his readiness to aid and
advise, if it could be of use to us, and to overcome any and every difficulty, was unequalled.
To Albert he showed the greatest kindness and
the utmost confidence. His experience and his
knowledge of the past were so great too; he was
a link which connected us with bygone times,
with the last century. Not an eye will be dry in
the whole country.

We hastened down on foot to the head of *Loch
Muich;* and then rode home, in a heavy shower,
to *Alt-na-Giuthasach.* Our whole enjoyment was
spoilt; a gloom overhung all of us.

We wrote to Lord Derby and Lord Charles
Wellesley.

BUILDING THE CAIRN ON CRAIG GOWAN, &c.

Monday, October 11, 1852.

This day has been a very happy, lucky, and memorable one—our last! A fine morning.

Albert had to see Mr. Walpole, and therefore it was nearly eleven o'clock before we could go up to the top of *Craig Gowan*, to see the cairn built, which was to commemorate our taking possession of this dear place; the old cairn having been pulled down. We set off with all the children, ladies, gentlemen, and a few of the servants, including Macdonald and Grant, who had not already gone up; and at the *Moss House*, which is half way, Mackay met us, and preceded us, playing, Duncan and Donald Stewart[*] going before

---

[*] One of the keepers, whom we found here in 1848. He is an excellent man, and was much liked by the Prince; he always led the dogs when the Prince went out stalking. He lives in the Western Lodge, close to Grant's house, which was built for him by the Prince.

him, to the highest point of *Craig Gowan ;* where
were assembled all the servants and tenants, with
their wives and children and old relations. All our
little friends were there : Mary Symons and Lizzie
Stewart, the four Grants, and several others.

I then placed the first stone, after which Albert
laid one, then the children, according to their ages.
All the ladies and gentlemen placed one ; and
then every one came forward at once, each person
carrying a stone and placing it on the cairn. Mr.
and Mrs. Anderson were there ; Mackay played ;
and whisky was given to all. It took, I am sure,
an hour building ; and whilst it was going on,
some merry reels were danced on a stone opposite. All the old people (even the gardener's
wife from *Corbie Hall,* near *Abergeldie,*) danced ;
and many of the children, Mary Symons and
Lizzie Stewart especially, danced so nicely ; the
latter with her hair all hanging down. Poor
dear old "Monk," Sir Robert Gordon's faithful
old dog, was sitting there amongst us all. At
last, when the cairn, which is, I think, seven
or eight feet high, was nearly completed, Albert
climbed up to the top of it, and placed the last
stone ; after which three cheers were given. It

was a gay, pretty, and touching sight; and I felt almost inclined to cry. The view was so beautiful over the dear hills; the day so fine; the whole so *gemüthlich*. May God bless this place, and allow us yet to see it and enjoy it many a long year!

After luncheon, Albert decided to walk through the wood for the last time, to have a last chance, and allowed Vicky and me to go with him. At half-past three o'clock we started, got out at Grant's, and walked up part of *Carrop*, intending to go along the upper path, when a stag was heard to roar, and we all turned into the wood. We crept along, and got into the middle path. Albert soon left us to go lower, and we sat down to wait for him; presently we heard a shot—then complete silence—and, after another pause of some little time, three more shots. This was again succeeded by complete silence. We sent some one to look, who shortly after returned, saying the stag had been twice hit and they were after him. Macdonald next went, and in about five minutes we heard "Solomon" give tongue, and knew he had the stag at bay. We listened a little while, and then began moving down hoping to arrive in time; but the barking had ceased, and Albert had already killed the stag; and on the road he lay, a little way beyond *Invergelder*—the beauty that we had admired yesterday evening. He was a magnificent animal, and I sat down and scratched a little sketch of him on a bit of paper that Macdonald had in his pocket, which I put on a stone—while Albert and Vicky, with the others, built a little

cairn to mark the spot. We heard, after I had finished my little scrawl, and the carriage had joined us, that another stag had been seen near the road; and we had not gone as far as the " Irons," *

* These "Irons" are the levers of an old saw-mill which was pulled down, and they were left there to be sold—between thirty and forty years ago—and have remained there ever since, not being considered worth selling, on account of the immense trouble of transporting them.

before we saw one below the road, looking so handsome. Albert jumped out and fired—the animal fell, but rose again, and went on a little way, and Albert followed. Very shortly after, however, we heard a cry, and ran down and found Grant and Donald Stewart pulling up a stag with a very pretty head. Albert had gone on, Grant went after him, and I and Vicky remained with Donald Stewart, the stag, and the dogs. I sat down to sketch, and poor Vicky, unfortunately, seated herself on a wasp's nest, and was much stung. Donald Stewart rescued her, for I could not, being myself too much alarmed. Albert joined us in twenty minutes, unaware of having killed the stag. What a delightful day! But sad that it should be the last day! Home by half-past six. We found our beautiful stag had arrived, and admired him much.

LAYING THE FOUNDATION STONE OF OUR NEW HOUSE.

September 28, 1853.

A fine morning early, but when we walked out at half-past ten o'clock it began raining, and soon poured down without ceasing. Most fortunately it cleared up before two, and the sun shone brightly for the ceremony of laying the foundation stone of the new house. Mama and all her party arrived from *Abergeldie* a little before three. I annex the Programme of the Ceremony, which was strictly adhered to, and was really very interesting :—

PROGRAMME.

The stone being prepared and suspended over that upon which it is to rest, (in which will be a cavity for the bottle containing the parchment and the coins):

The workmen will be placed in a semicircle at a little distance from the stone, and the women and home servants in an inner semicircle.

Her Majesty the Queen, and His Royal Highness the Prince, accompanied by the Royal Children, Her Royal Highness the Duchess of Kent, and attended by Her Majesty's guests and suite, will proceed from the house.

Her Majesty, the Prince, and the Royal Family, will stand on the South side of the stone, the suite being behind and on each side of the Royal party.

The Rev. Mr. Anderson will then pray for a blessing on the work. Her Majesty will affix her signature to the parchment, recording the day upon which the foundation stone was laid. Her Majesty's signature will be followed by that of the Prince and the Royal Children, the Duchess of Kent, and any others that Her Majesty may command, and the parchment will be placed in the bottle.

One of each of the current coins of the present reign will also be placed in the bottle, and the bottle having been sealed up, will be placed in the cavity. The trowel will then be delivered to Her Majesty by Mr. Smith of Aberdeen, the architect, and the mortar having been spread, the stone will be lowered.

The level and square will then be applied, and their correctness having been ascertained, the mallet will be delivered to Her Majesty by Mr. Stuart (the clerk of the works), when Her Majesty will strike the stone and declare it to be laid. The cornucopia will be placed upon the stone, and the oil and wine poured out by Her Majesty.

The pipes will play, and Her Majesty, with the Royal Family, will retire.

As soon after as it can be got ready, the workmen will proceed to their dinner. After dinner, the following toasts will be given by Mr. Smith :—

" The Queen."

"The Prince and the Royal Family."

"Prosperity to the house, and happiness to the inmates of Balmoral."

The workmen will then leave the dinner-room, and amuse themselves upon the green with Highland games till seven o'clock, when a dance will take place in the ball-room.

We walked round to the spot, preceded by Mackay. Mr. Anderson* made a very appropriate prayer. The wind was very high; but else everything went off as well as could possibly be desired.

The workmen and people all gave a cheer when the whole was concluded. In about three-quarters of an hour's time we went in to see the people at their dinner; and after this walked over to *Craig Gowan* for Albert to get a chance for black game.

We dressed early, and went for twenty minutes before dinner to see the people dancing in the ball-room, which they did with the greatest spirit.

* The Minister of Crathie: he died November, 1866.

THE KIRK.

October 29, 1854.

We went to Kirk, as usual, at twelve o'clock. The service was performed by the Rev. Norman McLeod, of *Glasgow*, son of Dr. McLeod, and anything finer I never heard. The sermon, entirely extempore, was quite admirable ; so simple, and yet so eloquent, and so beautifully argued and put. The text was from the account of the coming of Nicodemus to Christ by night ; St. John, chapter 3. Mr. McLeod showed in the sermon how we *all* tried to please *self,* and live for *that,* and in so doing found no rest. Christ had come not only to die for us, but to show how we were to live. The second prayer was very touching ; his allusions to us were so simple, saying, after his mention of us, " bless their children." It gave me a lump in my throat, as also when he prayed for "the dying, the wounded, the widow, and the orphans." Every one came back delighted; and how satisfactory it is to come back from church with such feelings! The servants and the Highlanders—*all*—were equally delighted.

Arrival at the New Castle at Balmoral.

September 7, 1855.

At a quarter-past seven o'clock we arrived at dear *Balmoral*. Strange, very strange, it seemed to me to drive past, indeed *through*, the old house; the connecting part between it and the offices being broken through. The new house looks beautiful. The tower and the rooms in the connecting part are, however, only .half finished, and the offices are still unbuilt: therefore the gentlemen (except the Minister *) live in the old house, and so do most of the servants; there is a long wooden passage which connects the new house with the offices. An old shoe was thrown after us into the house, for good luck, when we entered the hall. The house is charming; the rooms delightful; the furniture, papers, everything perfection.

* A Cabinet Minister is always in attendance upon the Queen at Balmoral.

IMPRESSIONS OF THE NEW CASTLE.

September 8, 1855.

The view from the windows of our rooms, and from the library, drawing-room, &c. below them, of the valley of the *Dee*, with the mountains in the background,—which one never could see from the old house, is quite beautiful. We walked about, and alongside the river, and looked at all that has been done, and considered all that has to be done; and afterwards we went over to the poor dear old house, and to our rooms, which it was quite melancholy to see so deserted; and settled about things being brought over.

News of the Fall of Sevastopol.

September 10, 1855.

Mama, and her lady and gentleman, to dinner.

All were in constant expectation of more telegraphic despatches. At half-past ten o'clock two arrived—one for me, and one for Lord Granville. I began reading mine, which was from Lord Clarendon, with details from Marshal Pélissier of the further destruction of the Russian ships; and Lord Granville said, "I have still better news;" on which he read, "From General Simpson—*Sevastopol is in the hands of the Allies.*" God be praised for it! Our delight was great; but we could hardly believe the good news, and from having so long, so anxiously expected it, one could not realize the actual fact.

Albert said they should go at once and light the bonfire which had been prepared when the false report of the fall of the town arrived last year, and had remained ever since, waiting to be lit. On the 5th of November, the day of the battle of *Inkermann*, the wind upset it, strange to say; and now again, most strangely, it only seemed to *wait* for our return to be lit.

The new house seems to be lucky, indeed; for, from the first moment of our arrival, we have had good news. In a few minutes, Albert and all the gentlemen, in every species of attire, sallied forth, followed by all the servants, and gradually by all the population of the village—keepers, gillies, workmen—up to the top of the cairn. We waited, and saw them light the bonfire; accompanied by general cheering. It blazed forth brilliantly, and we could see the numerous figures surrounding it —some dancing, all shouting;—Ross* playing his pipes, and Grant and Macdonald firing off guns continually; while poor old François d'Albert-ançon† lighted a number of squibs below, the greater part of which would not go off. About three-quarters of an hour after, Albert came

---

* My Piper since 1854; he had served seventeen years in the 42nd Highlanders—a very respectable, good man.

† An old servant of Sir R. Gordon's, who had charge of the house, and was a native of Alsace; he died in 1858.

down, and said the scene had been wild and exciting beyond everything. The people had been drinking healths in whisky, and were in great ecstasy. The whole house seemed in a wonderful state of excitement. The boys were with difficulty awakened, and when at last this was the case, they begged leave to go up to the top of the cairn.

We remained till a quarter to twelve; and, just as I was undressing, all the people came down under the windows, the pipes playing, the people singing, firing off guns, and cheering—first for me, then for Albert, the Emperor of the French, and the "downfall of *Sevastopol.*"

The Betrothal of the Princess Royal.

September 29, 1855.

Our dear Victoria was this day engaged to Prince Frederick William of Prussia, who had been on a visit to us since the 14th. He had already spoken to us, on the 20th, of his wishes; but we were uncertain, on account of her extreme youth, whether he should speak to her himself, or wait till he came back again. However, we felt it was better he should do so; and during our ride up *Craig-na-Ban* this afternoon, he picked a piece of white heather, (the emblem of "good luck,") which he gave to her; and this enabled him to make an allusion to his hopes and wishes, as they rode down *Glen Girnoch*, which led to this happy conclusion.

The Kirk.

October 14, 1855.

To Kirk at twelve o'clock. The Rev. J. Caird, one of the most celebrated preachers in *Scotland*, performed the service, and electrified all present by a most admirable and beautiful sermon, which lasted nearly an hour, but which kept one's attention riveted. The text was from the twelfth chapter of Romans, and the eleventh verse : " *Not slothful* " *in business ; fervent in spirit ; serving the Lord.*" He explained, in the most beautiful and simple manner, what real religion is ; how it ought to pervade every action of our lives; not a thing only for Sundays, or for our closet; not a thing to drive us from the world; not "a perpetual " moping over 'good' books," but "being and " doing good ;" "letting everything be done in a " Christian spirit." It was as fine as Mr. McLeod's sermon last year, and sent us home much edified.

FINDING THE OLD CASTLE GONE.

August 30, 1856.

On arriving at *Balmoral* at seven o'clock in the evening, we found the tower finished as well as the offices, and the poor old house gone! The effect of the whole is very fine.

Gardens, &c. round the New Castle.

August 31, 1856.

We walked along the river and outside the house. The new offices and the yard are excellent; and the little garden on the west side, with the eagle fountain which the King of Prussia gave me, and which used to be in the greenhouse at *Windsor*, is extremely pretty; as are also the flower-beds under the walls of the side which faces the *Dee*. There are sculptured arms on the different shields, gilt, which has a very good effect; and a bas-relief under our windows—not gilt—representing St. Hubert, with St. Andrew on one side and St. George on the other side: all done by Mr. Thomas.*

* He died in March, 1862. The Prince had a high opinion of his taste.

LOVE FOR BALMORAL.

October 13, 1856.

Every year my heart becomes more fixed in this dear Paradise, and so much more so now, that *all* has become my dearest Albert's *own* creation, own work, own building, own laying out, as at *Osborne;* and his great taste, and the impress of his dear hand, have been stamped everywhere. He was very busy to-day, settling and arranging many things for next year.

Opening of the New Bridge over the Linn of Dee.

September 8, 1857.

At half-past one o'clock we started in "Highland state,"—Albert in a royal Stuart plaid, and I and the girls in skirts of the same,—with the ladies (who had only returned at five in the morning from the ball at *Mar Lodge*) and gentlemen, for the *Linn of Dee*, to open the new bridge there. The valley looked beautiful. A triumphal arch was erected, at which Lord Fife and Mr. Brooke received us, and walked near the carriage, pipers playing—the road lined with Duff men. On the bridge Lady Fife received us, and we all drank in whisky "prosperity to the bridge." The view of the linn is very fine from it.

All the company and a band were outside a tent on the bank overlooking the bridge. Here we took some tea, talked with the company, and then drove back by *Mar Lodge*,—the Fifes preceding us to the end of the grounds. The same people were there as at the Gatherings,—the Campdens, Errolls, Airlies, old Lady Duff, and Mr. and Lady L. Brooke, and others. We were home at half-past five, not without having some rain by the way.

Visits to the Old Women.

Saturday, September 26, 1857.

Albert went out with Alfred for the day, and I walked out with the two girls and Lady Churchill, stopped at the shop and made some purchases for poor people and others; drove a little way, got out and walked up the hill to *Balnacroft*, Mrs. P. Farquharson's, and she walked round with us to some of the cottages to show me where the poor people lived, and to tell them who I was. Before we went into any we met an old woman, who, Mrs. Farquharson said, was very poor, eighty-eight years old, and mother to the former distiller. I gave her a warm petticoat, and the tears rolled down her old cheeks, and she shook my hands, and prayed God to bless me : it was very touching.

I went into a small cabin of old Kitty Kear's, who is eighty-six years old—quite erect, and who welcomed us with a great air of dignity. She sat down and spun. I gave her, also, a warm petticoat; she said, "May the Lord ever attend ye " and yours, here and hereafter; and may the " Lord be a guide to ye, and keep ye from all " harm." She was quite surprised at Vicky's height; great interest is taken in her. We went on to a cottage (formerly Jean Gordon's), to visit old widow Symons, who is "past fourscore," with a nice rosy face, but was bent quite double; she was most friendly, shaking hands with us all, asking which was I, and repeating many kind blessings: "May the Lord attend ye " with mirth and with joy; may He ever be with " ye in this world, and when ye leave it." To Vicky, when told she was going to be married, she said, "May the Lord be a guide to ye in " your future, and may every happiness attend " ye." She was very talkative; and when I said I hoped to see her again, she expressed an expectation that "she should be called any day," and so did Kitty Kear. *

We went into three other cottages: to Mrs. Symons's (daughter-in-law to the old widow living next door), who had an "unwell boy;" then

* She died in Jan. 1865.

across a little burn to another old woman's; and afterwards peeped into Blair the fiddler's. We drove back, and got out again to visit old Mrs. Grant (Grant's mother), who is so tidy and clean, and to whom I gave a dress and handkerchief, and she said, " You're too kind to me, you're " over kind to me, ye give me more every year, " and I get older every year." After talking some time with her, she said, " I am happy to see ye " looking so nice." She had tears in her eyes, and speaking of Vicky's going, said, " I'm very sorry, " and I think she is sorry hersel' ;" and, having said she feared she would not see her (the Princess) again, said : " I am very sorry I said that, " but I meant no harm; I always say just what I " think, not what is fut" (fit). Dear old lady; she is such a pleasant person.

Really the affection of these good people, who are so hearty and so happy to see you, taking interest in everything, is very touching and gratifying.

VISIT TO THE PRINCE'S ENCAMPMENT AT FEITHORT.

Tuesday, October 6, 1857.

At twelve o'clock I drove off with the two girls
to the " Irons," where we mounted our ponies,

and rode up (Brown and Robertson attending
on foot) through the *Corrie Buie*, along the
pretty new path through *Feithluie* to the foot of
the very steep ascent to *Feithort*, where we got

off and walked up—and suddenly, when nearly
at the top of the path, came upon Albert's little
encampment, which was just at the edge of the
winding path.

Albert was still absent, having gone out at
six o'clock, but Löhlein and some of the gillies
were there. The little house, with shelves for
keeping a few boxes (no seat), and a little stove,
was not at all uncomfortable; but the wind was
dreadfully high, and blew in. We waited for
about a quarter of an hour, and then Albert
arrived; he had been out since six o'clock, shot
three stags, but only got one bad one. The fine
one, yesterday evening, had cost him much trouble.
The night had been bitterly cold and windy; but
he had slept. We lunched in the little "housie"
at the open door. There was a second hut for
the people. Luncheon over, we walked down and
across the greater part of the *Balloch Buie*, mount-
ing our ponies wherever it was wet. We saw
deer as we came lower down, and all of a sudden
a stag was seen quite close by the path; Albert
shot him, and he fell at once. He had very fine
horns, a royal on one side.

Then they beat up to the *Craig Daign*. Poor

Albert was much tired, and had to walk all the time, as he had no pony; we rode part of the way. Then the lower part of the road was driven. As we were sitting by a tree close to Albert a stag came out, and Albert killed him at one shot. A fine day, though at times it has been very cold. We got home at half-past six.

A FALL OF SNOW.

September 18, 1858.

Alas! the last day! When we got up the weather seemed very hopeless. Everything was white with snow, which lay, at least, an inch on the ground, and it continued snowing heavily, as it had done since five this morning. I wished we might be snowed up, and unable to move. How happy I should have been could it have been so! It continued snowing till half-past ten or eleven, and then it began to clear up. The hills appeared quite white; the sun came out, and it became splendidly bright. Albert was going to have the woods driven—which are not properly called *Carrop Woods*, but *Garmaddie Woods*— but had first to ride round *Craig Gowan* with Dr Robertson to see *Robrech*, the place where

Duncan's new house is to be built, which is above the village, opposite *Craig Luraghain*, with a most splendid view ; and at Grant's house I was to meet him.

At one o'clock I left with Alice and Lenchen[*] for Grant's, where we met Albert, who joined us in the carriage : the day was truly splendid. We got out at the river, and were going down to *Nelly's Bush*, when a stag was heard roaring very near ; so we had to stop, and, with our plaids and cloaks to sit upon, really avoided getting very wet. We waited till Albert was near to the stag, saw it move, heard Albert fire twice, and the stag turn, stop, and then disappear. Albert fired again, but the stag had crossed the *Dee;* so we turned up on to the road, and went into the dear old *Corrie Buie;* Albert turning off to see if there were any deer near, while we waited for him. We then came to a place which is always wet, but which was particularly bad after the late rain and snow. There was no pony for me to get on ; and as I wished not to get my feet wet by walking through the long grass, Albert proposed I should be carried over in a plaid ; and

[*] Princess Helena.

Lenchen was first carried over; but it was held too low, and her feet dangled; so Albert suggested the plaid should be put round the men's shoulders, and that I should sit upon it; Brown and Duncan, the two strongest and handiest, were the two who undertook it, and I sat safely enough with an arm on each man's shoulder, and was carried successfully over. All the Highlanders are so amusing, and really pleasant and instructive to talk to—women as well as men—and the latter so gentlemanlike.* Albert's shots were

---

* A similar view to that given in the text is admirably expressed by the Reverend Frederick W. Robertson in his *Lectures on Literary and Social Topics*, and his description of a Tyrolese is even more applicable to a Highlander.

" My companion was a Tyrolese chamois-hunter, a man who, in point of social position, might rank with an English labourer. I fear there would be a difficulty in England in making such a companionship pleasurable and easy to both parties; there would be a painful obsequiousness, or else an insolent familiarity on the one side, constraint on the other. In this case there was nothing of that sort. We walked together, and ate together. He had all the independence of a man, but he knew the courtesy which was due to a stranger; and when we parted for the night, he took his leave with a politeness and dignity which would have done no discredit to the most finished gentleman. The reason, as it seemed to me, was that his character had been moulded by the sublimities of the forms of the out-heard close by whilst we were at luncheon; and there was a general rush of all the people. Albert joined us soon after; he had had a great deal of trouble in stalking his stag, which he had been after several days, but had killed him at one shot. He was brought for us to see: a very light-coloured one, with fine straight horns, of extraordinary thickness. After this we walked on for a beat quite round *Carrop;* and the view was glorious! A little shower of snow had fallen, but was succeeded by brilliant sunshine. The hills covered with snow, the golden birch-trees on the lower brown hills, and the

ward nature amidst which he lived. It was impossible to see the clouds wreathing themselves in that strange wild way of theirs round the mountain crests, till the hills seemed to become awful things, instinct with life—it was impossible to walk, as we did sometimes, an hour or two before sunrise, and see the morning's beams gilding with their pure light the grand old peaks on the opposite side of the valley, while we ourselves were still in deepest shade, and look on that man, his very exterior in harmony with all around him, and his calm eye resting on all that wondrous spectacle, without a feeling that these things had had their part in making him what he was, and that you were in a country in which men were bound to be polished, bound to be more refined, almost bound to be better men than elsewhere."

bright afternoon sky, were indescribably beautiful.
The following lines * admirably pourtray what I
then saw :—

"The gorgeous bright October,
Then when brackens are changed, and heather blooms are
    faded,
And amid russet of heather and fern, green trees are bonnie;
Alders are green, and oaks; the rowan scarlet and yellow;
One great glory of broad gold pieces appears the aspen,
And the jewels of gold that were hung in the hair of the
    birch-tree,
Pendulous, here and there, her coronet, necklace, and ear-
    rings,
Cover her now, o'er and o'er; she is weary and scatters them
    from her."

Oh! how I gazed and gazed on God's glorious
works with a sad heart, from its being for the last
time, and tried to carry the scene away, well
-implanted and fixed in my mind, for this effect
with the snow we shall not often see again. We
saw it like this in 1852 ; but we have not seen it
so since, though we have often had snow-storms
and showers with a little snow lying on the
highest hills.

* *The Bothie of Tober-na-Vuolich.* By Arthur Hugh Clough.

ASCENT OF MORVEN.

September 14, 1859.

I felt very low-spirited at my dearest Albert having to leave at one o'clock for *Aberdeen*, to preside at the meeting of the British Association.

I with Alice, the two ladies, Lord Charles Fitzroy, and Brown, left shortly before for *Morven*. We took post-horses at the foot of *Gairn*, and drove by the right side of the glen, along a new good road, avoiding the ford, and by half-past two we were at the foot of *Morven*, not far from the shooting-lodge there. Here we mounted our ponies, and our caravan started with the gillies —Jemmie Coutts, an old acquaintance, now keeper at the lodge, leading the way. About half-way, at a burn-side, we stopped, seated ourselves on plaids on the fine springy turf, and took luncheon ; then walked about, sketched, mounted our ponies, and rode up to the top, which was rather steep and soft,—"foggy," as Brown called it, which is the Highland expression for mossy, —my little pony, being so fat, panted dreadfully. *Morven* is 2,700 feet high, and the view from it more magnificent than can be described, so large and yet so near everything seemed, and such seas of mountains with blue lights, and the colour so wonderfully beautiful. We looked down upon the Duke of Richmond's property, and saw the mountain called the *Buck of Cabrach*, and still further on the *Slate Hills;* to the east, *Aberdeen* and the blue sea, and we could even see the ships with the naked eye: the table-land between *Tarland* and *Ballater;* and stretching out below, due south, *Mount Keen.* To the south-west, *Loch-na-Gar;* to the west, *Ben A'an* and *Ben-na-Bhourd,*—"the land of *Gairn,*" as they call it, —and *Muich;* and *Deeside* in the foreground. It was enchanting! We walked down to where we had lunched, and rode to the bottom. Here we found a fire, also tea with cakes, &c., which had been very kindly prepared for us by a lady and gentleman, the daughter and son of Sir J. G. Ratcliff, living in the shooting-lodge.

We drank the tea, and left in the carriage at half-past six o'clock, reaching *Balmoral* at half-past seven. So sad not to find my darling Husband at home.

THE PRINCE'S RETURN FROM ABERDEEN.

September 15, 1859.

I heard by telegram last night that Albert's reception was admirable, and that all was going off as well as possible. Thank God. I ascended *Loch-na-Gar* with Alice, Helena, Bertie, Lady Churchill, Colonel Bruce, and our usual attendants, and returned after six o'clock. At ten minutes past seven arrived my beloved Albert. All had gone off most admirably; he had seen many learned people; all were delighted with his speech; the reception most gratifying. *Banchory House* (Mr. Thomson's) where he lodged (four miles from *Aberdeen*) was, he said, very comfortable.

Féte to the Members of the British Association.

———

September 22, 1859.

The morning dawned brightly. Suddenly a very high wind arose which alarmed us, but yet it looked bright, and we hoped the wind would keep off the rain; but after breakfast, while watching the preparations, showers began, and from half-past eleven a fearful down-pour, with that white curtain-like appearance which is so alarming; and this lasted till half-past twelve. I was in despair; but at length it began to clear, just as the neighbours with their families, and some of the farmers opposite (the Herrons, Duncans, Brown's father and brothers) arrived, and then came the huge omnibuses and carriages laden with "philosophers." At two o'clock we were all ready. Albert and the boys were in their kilts, and I and the girls in royal Stuart skirts and shawls over black velvet bodies.

It was a beautiful sight in spite of the frequent slight showers which at first tormented us,
and the very high cold wind. There were
gleams of sunshine, which, with the Highlanders
in their brilliant and picturesque dresses, the
wild notes of the pipes, the band, and the beautiful background of mountains, rendered the
scene wild and striking in the extreme. The
Farquharson's men headed by Colonel Farquharson, the Duff's by Lord Fife, and the Forbes's
men by Sir Charles Forbes, had all marched on
the ground before we came out, and were drawn
up just opposite to us, and the spectators (the
people of the country) behind them. We stood
on the terrace, the company near us, and the
"savants," also, on either side of us, and along
the slopes, on the grounds. The games began
about three o'clock :

     1. " Throwing the Hammer."
     2. " Tossing the Caber."
     3. " Putting the Stone."

We gave prizes to the three best in each
of the games. We walked along the terrace
to the large marquee, talking to the people, to

where the men were "putting the stone." After
this returned to the upper terrace, to see the
race, a pretty wild sight; but the men looked
very cold, with nothing but their shirts and kilts
on; they ran beautifully. They wrapped plaids
round themselves, and then came to receive the
prizes from me. Last of all came the dancing—
reels and "Ghillie Callum." The latter the judges
could not make up their minds about; it was
danced over and over again; and at last they left
out the best dancer of all! They said he danced
"too well!" The dancing over, we left amid the
loud cheers of the people. It was then about
half-past five. We watched from the window
the Highlanders marching away, the different
people walking off, and four weighty omnibuses
filling with the scientific men. We saw, and
talked to, Professor Owen, Sir David Brewster,
Sir John Bowring, Mr. J. Roscoe, and Sir John
Ross.*

When almost all were gone, we took a short walk

---

* During the Fête, we heard from Sir R. Murchison and
others that news had been received this morning of the finding
of poor Sir John Franklin's remains—or, rather, of the things
belonging to him and his party.

to warm ourselves. Much pleased at everything having gone off well. The Duke of Richmond, Sir R. Murchison, General Sabine, Mr. Thomson of *Banchory House*, and Professor Phillipps, Secretary of the Association, all of whom slept here, were additions to the dinner-party. I sat between our cousin Philip (Count of Flanders) and the Duke of Richmond. All the gentlemen spoke in very high terms of my beloved Albert's admirable speech, the good it had done, and the general satisfaction it had caused.

We could see the fire of the Forbes's encampment on the opposite side.

EXPEDITION TO INCHRORY.

September 30, 1859.

At twenty minutes past eleven we started with Helena and Louise in the sociable, Grant on the box, for *Loch Bulig*, passing the farms of *Blairglass* and of *Dall Dounie*, and the shooting-lodge of *Corndavon*, ten miles distant. Here we found our ponies (mine being " Victoria"), and rode along the edge of the lake, up a beautiful glen, by a path winding through the valley, which appeared frequently closed. We then rode along a small river or burn, of which no one knew the name ; none of our party having ever been there before. The hills were sprinkled with birch-trees, and there was grass below in the valley ; we saw deer. As we approached *Inchrory* (a shooting-lodge of Lord H. Bentinck's) the scenery became finer and finer, reminding us of *Glen Tilt*, and was most beautiful at *Inchrory*, with the fine broad water of the *Avon* flowing down from the mountains.

We inquired of the people at *Inchrory* whether there was any way of getting round over the hills by *Gairn Shiel*, and they said there was; but that the distance was about 11 miles. Neither Grant nor Brown had been that way. However we accepted it at once, and I was delighted to go on *à l'improviste*, travelling about in these enchanting hills in this solitude, with only our good Highlanders with us, who never make difficulties, but are cheerful, and happy, and merry, and ready to walk, and run, and do anything. So on we went, turning up above *Inchrory* by a winding road between hillocks and commanding a glorious view towards *Laganaul*. Here, on a little grassy knoll, we lunched in a splendid position.

After our luncheon, and walking a little way, we remounted, and proceeded by the so-called "Brown Cow" (on the other side of which we had driven,) over a moor, meeting a shepherd, out of whom Grant could get little information. Soon we came to corn-fields in the valley; passed *Favanché* and *Inchmore*, and got on to a good road, on which Brown and Grant "travelled" at a *wonderful* pace, upwards of five miles an hour without stopping ; and the former with that vigorous, light, elastic tread which is quite astonishing. We passed *Dal-na-Damph Shiel* (a shooting-lodge of Sir Charles Forbes) ; and went along the old " Military Road," leaving *Cockbridge*, a small straggling " toun," which is on the road to *Inverness*, to our left, and the old *Castle of Corgarf* to our right. We looked over into *Donside*. The road was soon left for a mountain one in the hills, above one of the tributary streams of the *Don*, and was wild and desolate ; we passed *Dal Choupar* and *Dal Vown*, and, as we ascended we saw *Tornahoish*, at a distance to the left. After going along this hill-track, over some poor and tottering bridges, we joined the road by which we had driven to *Tornahoish*. It was fast getting dark, but was very fine. I and the girls got off and walked sharply some little distance. Albert had walked further on, Grant riding his pony meantime. P. Robertson and Kennedy, besides those I have named, carried the basket alternately.

We remounted our ponies, and Brown led mine on at an amazing pace up the *Glaschoil Hill*, and we finally reached *Gairn Shiel* after seven, quite in the dark. There, at the small public-house, we found the carriage, and drove off as soon as we could; the ponies were to be given half a feed, and then to come on. We had to drive home very slowly, as the road is not good, and very steep in parts.

A mild night. Home by ten minutes past eight, enchanted with our day. How I wish we could travel about in this way, and see *all* the wild spots in the *Highlands!* We had gone 35 miles, having ridden 19 and a half! The little girls were in great glee the whole time.

ASCENT OF BEN MUICH DHUI.

Friday, October 7, 1859.

Breakfast at half-past eight. At ten minutes to nine we started, in the sociable, with Bertie and Alice and our usual attendants. Drove along the opposite side of the river. The day very mild and promising to be fine, though a little heavy over the hills, which we anxiously watched. At *Castleton* we took four post-horses, and drove to the *Shiel of the Derry*, that beautiful spot where we were last year—which Albert had never seen—and arrived there just before eleven. Our ponies were there with Kennedy, Robertson, and Jemmie Smith. One pony carried the luncheon-baskets. After all the cloaks, &c. had been placed on the ponies, or carried by the men, we mounted and began our "journey." I was on "Victoria," Alice on "Dobbins." George McHardy, an elderly man who knew the country (and acts as a guide, carrying luggage for people across the hills "on beasts" which he keeps for that purpose), led the way. We rode (my pony being led by Brown most of the time both going up and down) at least four miles up *Glen Derry*, which is very fine, with the remnants of a splendid forest, *Cairn Derry* being to the right, and the *Derry Water* running below. The track was very bad and stony, and broken up by cattle coming down for the "Tryst." At the end of the glen we crossed a ford, passed some softish ground, and turned up to the left by a very rough, steep, but yet gradual ascent to *Corrie Etchan*, which is in a very wild rugged spot, with magnificent precipices, a high mountain to the right called *Ben Main*, while to the left was *Cairngorm of Derry*. When we reached the top of this very steep ascent (we had been rising, though almost imperceptibly, from the *Derry Shiel*), we came upon a loch of the same name, which reminded us of *Loch-na-Gar* and of *Loch-na-Nian*. You look from here on to other wild hills and corries—on *Ben A'an*, &c. We ascended very gradually, but became so enveloped in mist that we could see nothing— hardly those just before us! Albert had walked a good deal; and it was very cold. The mist got worse; and as we rode along the stony, but almost flat ridge of *Ben Muich Dhui*, we hardly knew whether we were on level ground or the top of the mountain. However, I and Alice rode to the very top, which we reached a few minutes past two; and here, at a cairn of stones, we lunched, in a piercing cold wind.

Just as we sat down, a gust of wind came and dispersed the mist, which had a most wonderful effect, like a dissolving view—and exhibited the grandest, wildest scenery imaginable! We sat on a ridge of the cairn to take our luncheon,—our good people being grouped with the ponies near us. Luncheon over, Albert ran off with Alice to the ridge to look at the splendid view, and sent for me to follow. I did so; but not without Grant's help, for there were quantities of large loose stones heaped up together to walk upon. The wind was fearfully high, but the view was well worth seeing. I cannot describe all, but we saw where the *Dee* rises between the mountains called the *Well of Dee—Ben-y-Ghlo*—and the adjacent mountains, *Ben Vrackie*—then *Ben-na-Bhourd—Ben A'an*, &c.—and such magnificent

wild rocks, precipices, and corries. It had
a sublime and solemn effect; so wild, so solitary—no one but ourselves and our little party
there.

Albert went on further with the children, but I
returned with Grant to my seat on the cairn, as I
could not scramble about well. Soon after, we
all began walking and looking for " cairngorms,"
and found some small ones. The mist had
entirely cleared away below, so that we saw all
the beautiful views. *Ben Muich Dhui* is 4,297
feet high, one of the highest mountains in *Scotland.* I and Alice rode part of the way, walking
wherever it was very steep. Albert and Bertie
walked the whole time. I had a little whisky
and water, as the people declared pure water
would be too chilling. We then rode on without
getting off again, Albert talking so gaily with
Grant. Upon which Brown observed to me in
simple Highland phrase, " It's very pleasant to
" walk with a person who is always 'content.' "
Yesterday, in speaking of dearest Albert's sport,
when I observed he never was cross after bad
luck, Brown said, " Every one on the estate says
" there never was so kind a master; I am sure

" our only wish is to give satisfaction." I said, they certainly did.*

By a quarter-past six o'clock we got down to the *Shiel of the Derry*, where we found some tea, which we took in the " shiel,"† and started again by moonlight at about half-past six. We reached *Castleton* at half-past seven—and after this it became cloudy. At a quarter-past eight precisely we were at *Balmoral*, much delighted and not at all tired; everything had been so well arranged, and so quietly, without any fuss. *Never* shall I forget this day, or the impression this very grand scene made upon me; truly sublime and impressive; such solitude!

* We were always in the habit of conversing with the Highlanders—with whom one comes so much in contact in the Highlands. The Prince highly appreciated the good-breeding, simplicity, and intelligence, which make it so pleasant, and even instructive to talk to them.

† " Shiel " means a small shooting-lodge.

FIRST GREAT EXPEDITION :—To GLEN FISHIE

AND GRANTOWN.

Hotel Grantown,
Tuesday, September 4, 1860.

Arrived this evening after a most interesting tour; I will recount the events of the day. Breakfasted at *Balmoral* in our own room at half-past seven o'clock, and started at eight or a little past, with Lady Churchill and General Grey, in the sociable (Grant and Brown on the box as usual) for *Castleton,* where we changed horses. We went on five miles beyond the *Linn of Dee,* to the *Shepherd's Shiel of Geldie,* or, properly speaking, *Giuly,* where we found our ponies and a guide, Charlie Stewart. We mounted at once, and rode up along the *Geldie,* which we had to ford frequently to avoid the bogs, and rode on for two hours up *Glen Geldie,* over a moor which was so soft and boggy in places, that we had to get off several times. The hills were wild, but not very high, bare of trees, and even of heather to a great extent, and not picturesque till we approached the *Fishie*, and turned to the right up to the glen which we could see in the distance. The *Fishie* and *Geldie* rise almost on a level, with very little distance between them. The *Fishie* is a fine rapid stream, full of stones. As you approach the glen, which is very narrow, the scenery becomes very fine—particularly after fording the *Etchart*, a very deep ford. Grant, on his pony, led me through : our men on foot took off their shoes and stockings to get across. From this point the narrow path winds along the base of the hills of *Craig-na-Go'ar*—the rocks of the "Goat Craig ;"—*Craig-na-Caillach;* and *Stron-na-Barin*—"the nose of the queen." The rapid river is overhung by rocks, with trees, birch and fir ; the hills, as you advance, rise very steeply on both sides, with rich rocks and corries, and occasional streamlets falling from very high— while the path winds along, rising gradually higher and higher. It is quite magnificent!

We stopped when we came to a level spot amongst the trees. The native firs are particularly fine ; and the whole is grand in the

extreme. We lunched here—a charming spot—
at two o'clock; and then pursued our journey.
We walked on a little way to where the valley
and glen widen out, and where there is what they
call here a green "hard." We got on our ponies
again and crossed the *Fishie* (a stream we forded
many times in the course of the day) to a place
where the finest fir-trees are, amidst some of the
most beautiful scenery possible.

Then we came upon a most lovely spot—the
scene of all Landseer's glory—and where there is
a little encampment of wooden and turf huts, built
by the late Duchess of Bedford; now no longer
belonging to the family, and, alas! all falling into
decay—among splendid fir-trees, the mountains
rising abruptly from the sides of the valley. We
were quite enchanted with the beauty of the
view. This place is about seven miles from the
mouth of the *Fishie*. Emerging from the wood
we came upon a good road, with low hills, beautifully heather-coloured, to the left; those to the
right, high and wooded, with noble corries and
waterfalls.

We met Lord and Lady Alexander Russell at
a small farm-house, just as we rode out of the

wood, and had some talk with them. They feel deeply the ruin of the place where they formerly lived, as it no longer belongs to them. We rode on for a good long distance, 12 miles, till we came to the ferry of the *Spey*. Deer were being driven in the woods, and we heard several shots. We saw fine ranges of hills on the *Spey-side*, or *Strathspey*, and opening to our left, those near *Loch Laggan*. We came to a wood of larch; from that, upon cultivated land, with *Kinrara* towards our right, where the monument to the late Duke of Gordon is conspicuously seen on a hill, which was perfectly crimson with heather.

Before entering the larch wood, Lord Alexander Russell caught us up again in a little pony carriage, having to go the same way, and he was so good as to explain everything to us. He showed us " The Duke of Argyll's Stone "—a cairn on the top of a hill to our right, celebrated, as seems most probable, from the Marquis of Argyll having halted there with his army. We came to another larch wood, when I and Lady Churchill got off our ponies, as we were very stiff from riding so long; and at the end of this wood we came upon *Loch Inch*, which is lovely, and of which I

should have liked exceedingly to have taken a
sketch, but we were pressed for time and hurried.
The light was lovely; and some cattle were
crossing a narrow strip of grass across the end
of the loch nearest to us, which really made a
charming picture. It is not a wild lake, quite
the contrary; no high rocks, but woods and
blue hills as a background. About a mile from
this was the ferry. There we parted from
our ponies, only Grant and Brown coming on
with us. Walker, the police inspector, met us,
but did not keep with us. He had been sent to
order everything in a quiet way, without letting

people suspect who we were : in this he entirely
succeeded. The ferry was a very rude affair; it

was like a boat or coble, but we could only stand on it, and it was moved at one end by two long oars, plied by the ferryman and Brown, and at the other end by a long sort of beam, which Grant took in hand. A few seconds brought us over to the road, where there were two shabby vehicles, one a kind of barouche, into which Albert and I got, Lady Churchill and General Grey into the other— a break; each·with a pair of small and rather miserable horses, driven by a man from the box. Grant was on our carriage, and Brown on the other. We had gone so far 40 miles, at least 20 on horseback. We had decided to call ourselves *Lord and Lady Churchill and party*, Lady Churchill passing as *Miss Spencer*, and General Grey as *Dr. Grey!* Brown once forgot this, and called me "Your Majesty" as I was getting into the carriage; and Grant on the box once called Albert "Your Royal Highness;" which set us off laughing, but no one observed it.

We had a long three hours' drive; it was six o'clock when we got into the carriage. We were soon out of the wood, and came upon the *Badenoch* road—passing close by *Kinrara*, but unfortunately not through it, which we ought to have done. It was very beautiful — fine wooded hills — the high *Cairngorm* range, and *Ben Muich Dhui*, unfortunately much obscured by the mist on the top—and the broad *Spey* flowing in the valley, with cultivated fields and fine trees below. Most striking, however, on our whole long journey was the utter, and to me very refreshing, solitude. Hardly a habitation! and hardly meeting a soul! It gradually grew dark. We stopped at a small half-way house for the horses to take some water; and the few people about stared vacantly at the two simple vehicles.

The mountains gradually disappeared,—the evening was mild, with a few drops of rain. On and on we went, till at length we saw lights, and drove through a long and straggling "toun," and turned down a small court to the door of the inn. Here we got out quickly—Lady Churchill and General Grey not waiting for us. We went up a small staircase, and were shown to our bed-room at the top of it—very small, but clean—with a large four-post bed which nearly filled the whole room. Opposite was the drawing and dining-room in one —very tidy and well-sized. Then came the room where Albert dressed, which was very small. The two maids (Jane Shackle * was with me) had driven over by another road in the waggonette, Stewart driving them. Made ourselves " clean and tidy," and then sat down to our dinner. Grant and Brown were to have waited on us, but were "bashful" and did not. A ringletted woman did everything; and, when dinner was over, removed the cloth and placed the bottle of wine (our own which we had brought) on the table with the glasses, which was the old English fashion. The dinner was very fair, and all very clean :—soup, "hodge-podge," mutton-broth with vegetables, which I did not much relish, fowl with white sauce, good roast lamb, very good potatoes, besides one or two other dishes, which I did not taste, ending with a good tart of cranberries. After dinner, I tried to write part of this account (but the talking round me confused me), while Albert played at " patience." Then went away, to begin undressing, and it was about half-past eleven, when we got to bed.

* One of my wardrobe-maids, and daughter to the Page mentioned earlier.

Wednesday, September 5.

A misty, rainy morning. Had not slept very soundly. We got up rather early, and sat working and reading in the drawing-room till the breakfast was ready, for which we had to wait some little time. Good tea and bread and butter, and some excellent porridge. Jane Shackle (who was very useful and attentive) said that they had all supped together, namely, the two maids, and Grant, Brown, Stewart, and Walker (who was still there), and were very merry in the "commercial room." The people were very amusing about us. The woman came in while they were at their dinner, and said to Grant, "Dr. Grey wants you," which nearly upset the gravity of all the others : then they told Jane, "Your lady gives no trouble;" and Grant in the morning called up to Jane, "Does his lordship want me ?" One could look on the street, which is a very long wide one, with detached houses, from our window. It was perfectly quiet, no one stirring, except here and there a man driving a cart, or a boy going along on his errand. General Grey bought himself a watch in a shop for 2*l.* !

At length, at about ten minutes to ten o'clock, we started in the same carriages and the same way as yesterday, and drove up to *Castle Grant*, Lord Seafield's place,—a fine (not Highland-looking) park, with a very plain-looking house, like a factory, about two miles from the town. It was drizzling almost the whole time. We did not get out, but drove back, having to pass through *Grantown* again ; where evidently " the murder was out," for all the people were in the street, and the landlady waved her pocket-handkerchief, and the ringletted maid (who had curl-papers in the morning) waved a flag from the window. Our coachman evidently did not observe or guess anything. As we drove out of the town, turning to our right through a wood, we met many people coming into the town, which the coachman said was for a funeral. We passed over the *Spey*, by the *Bridge of Spey*. It continued provokingly rainy, the mist hanging very low on the hills, which, however, did not seem to be very high, but were pink with heather. We stopped to have the cover of leather put over our carriage, which is the fashion of all the flys here. It keeps out the rain, however, very well.

The first striking feature in this country is

the *Pass of Dal Dhu*, above which the road
winds, — a steep corrie, with green hills. We
stopped at a small inn, with only one other house
near it; and here the poor wretchedly-jaded horses
got a little water, and waited for about ten minutes.
Further on we came to a very steep hill, also to a
sort of pass, called *Glen Bruin*, with green hills,
evidently of slate formation. Here we got out,
and walked down the hill, and over the *Bridge of
Bruin*, and partly up another hill, the road winding
amazingly after this—up and down hill. We then
came in sight of the *Avon*, winding below the hills;
and again got out at a little wood, before the *Bridge
of Avon;* the river is fine and clear here. We
re-entered our carriages (Lady Churchill and I for
this short time together), and drove about a mile
further up a hill to *Tomintoul;* our poor horses
being hardly able to drag themselves any longer,
the man whipping them and whistling to them to
go on, which they could not, and I thought every
instant that they would stop in the village. We
took four hours to drive these 14 miles ; for it
was two o'clock when we were outside the town,
and got out to mount our ponies. *Tomintoul*
is the most tumble-down, poor-looking place I

ever saw—a long street with three inns, miserable
dirty-looking houses and people, and a sad look
of wretchedness about it. Grant told me that it
was the dirtiest, poorest village in the whole of
the *Highlands*.

We mounted our ponies a short way out of
the town, but only rode for a few minutes as
it was past two o'clock. We came upon a
beautiful view, looking down upon the *Avon* and
up a fine glen. There we rested and took
luncheon. While Brown was unpacking and
arranging our things, I spoke to him and to
Grant, who was helping, about not having waited
on us, as they ought to have done, at dinner last
night and at breakfast, as we had wished ; and
Brown answered, he was afraid he should not do
it rightly ; I replied we did not wish to have
a stranger in the room, and they must do so
another time.

Luncheon (provisions for which we had taken
with us from home yesterday) finished, we
started again, walked a little way, till we were
overtaken by the men and ponies, and then
rode along *Avonside*, the road winding at the
bottom of the glen, which is in part tolerably

wide; but narrows as it turns, and winds round towards *Inchrory*, where it is called *Glen Avon*. The hills, sloping down to the river side, are beautifully green. It was very muggy—quite oppressive, and the greater part of the road deep and sloppy, till we came upon the granite formation again. In order to get on, as it was late, and we had eight miles to ride, our men,— at least Brown and two of the others,—walked before us at a fearful pace, so that we had to trot to keep up at all. Grant rode frequently on the deer pony; the others seemed, however, a good deal tired with the two long days' journey, and were glad to get on Albert's or the General's pony to give themselves a lift; but their willingness, readiness, cheerfulness, indefatigableness, are very admirable, and make them most delightful servants. As for Grant and Brown they are perfect — discreet, careful, intelligent, attentive, ever ready to do what is wanted; and the latter, particularly, is handy and willing to do everything and anything, and to overcome every difficulty, which makes him one of my best servants anywhere.

We passed by *Inchrory*—seeing, as we approached, two eagles towering splendidly above, and alighting on the top of the hills. From *Inchrory* we rode to *Loch Bulig*, which was beautifully lit up by the setting sun. From *Tomantoul* we escaped all real rain, having only a slight sprinkling every now and then. At *Loch Bulig* we found our carriage and four ponies, and drove back just as we left yesterday morning, reaching *Balmoral* safely at half-past seven.

What a delightful, successful expedition! Dear Lady Churchill was, as usual, thoroughly amiable, cheerful, and ready to do everything. Both she and the General seemed entirely to enjoy it, and enter into it, and so I am sure did our people. To my dear Albert do we owe it, for he always thought it would be delightful, having gone on many similar expeditions in former days himself. He enjoyed it very much. We heard since that the secret came out through a man recognizing Albert in the street yesterday morning; then the crown on the dog-cart made them think that it was some one from *Balmoral*, though they never suspected that it could be ourselves! "The lady must be terrible rich," the woman observed, as I had so many gold rings on my fingers!—I told

Lady Churchill she. had on many more than I had. When they heard who it was, they were ready to drop with astonishment and fright. I fear I have but poorly recounted this very amusing and never to be forgotten expedition, which will always be remembered with delight.

I must pay a tribute to our ponies. Dear " Fyvie " is perfection, and Albert's equally excellent.

SECOND GREAT EXPEDITION :—TO INVERMARK AND FETTERCAIRN.

Friday, September 20, 1861.

Looked anxiously at the weather at seven o'clock—there had been a little rain, there was still mist on the hills, and it looked doubtful. However, Albert said it would be best to keep to the original arrangements, and so we got up early, and by eight the sun shone, and the mist began to lift everywhere. We breakfasted at half-past eight, and at half-past nine we started in two sociables—Alice and Louis * with us in the first, and Grant on the box; Lady Churchill and General Grey in the second, and Brown on the box. We drove to the *Bridge of Muich*, where we found our six ponies, and five gillies, (J. Smith, J. Morgan, Kennedy, C. Stewart, and

* Prince Louis of Hesse.

S. Campbell.) We rode up the peat-road over the hill of *Polach* and down it again for about four miles, and then came to a very soft bit; but still with careful management we avoided getting into any of the bogs, and I remained on my pony all the time. Albert and Louis had to get off and walk for about two hundred yards. The hills of *Loch-na-Gar* were very hazy, but *Mount Keen* was in great beauty before us, and as we came down to the *Glen of Corrie Vruach*, and looked down *Glen Tanar*, the scenery was grand and wild. *Mount Keen* is a curious conical-shaped hill, with a deep corrie in it. It is nearly 3,200 feet high, and we had a very steep rough ascent over the shoulder, after crossing the *Tanar Water*. It was six and a half miles from the *Bridge of Muich* to *Corrie Vruach*.

When we were on the level ground again, where it was hard and dry, we all got off and walked on over the shoulder of the hill. We had not gone far when we descried Lord Dalhousie (whom General Grey had in confidence informed of our coming) on a pony. He welcomed us on the border of his " March," got off his pony and walked with us. After walking some little time Alice and I remounted our ponies, (Albert riding some part of the time,) and turned to the left, when we came in sight of a new country, and looked down a very fine glen— *Glen Mark.* We descended by a very steep but winding path, called *The Ladder*, very grand and wild : the water running through it is called *The Ladder Burn.* It is very fine indeed, and very striking. There is a small forester's lodge at the very foot of it. The pass is quite a narrow one ; you wind along a very steep and rough path, but still it was quite easy to ride on it, as it zigzags along. We crossed the burn at the bottom, where a picturesque group of " shearers " were seated, chiefly women, the older ones smoking. They were returning from the south to the north, whence they came. We rode up to the little cottage ; and in a little room of a regular Highland cabin, with its usual " press bed," we had luncheon. This place is called *Invermark*, and is four and a half miles from *Corrie Vruach.* After luncheon I sketched the fine view. The steep hill we came down immediately opposite the keeper's lodge is called *Craig Boestock*, and a very fine isolated craggy

hill which rises to the left—over-topping a small
and wild glen—is called the *Hill of Doun.*

We mounted our ponies a little after three, and
rode down *Glen Mark,* stopping to drink some
water out of a very pure well, called *The White
Well;* and crossing the *Mark* several times. As
we approached the *Manse of Loch Lee,* the glen
widened, and the old *Castle of Invermark* came
out extremely well ; and, surrounded by woods and
corn-fields, in which the people were "shearing,"
looked most picturesque. We turned to the right,
and rode up to the old ruined castle, which is half
covered with ivy. We then rode up to Lord
Dalhousie's shooting-lodge, where we dismounted.
It is a new and very pretty house, built of
granite, in a very fine position overlooking the
glen, with wild hills at the back. Miss Maule
(now Lady C. Maule) was there. We passed
through the drawing-room, and went on a few
yards to the end of a walk whence you see *Loch
Lee,* a wild, but not large, lake closed in by
mountains—with a farm-house and a few cottages
at its edge. The hall and dining-room are very
prettily fitted up with trophies of sport, and
the walls panelled with light wood. We had

a few of the very short showers which hung about the hills. We then got into our carriages. The carriage we were in was a sort of double dog-cart which could carry eight—but was very narrow inside. We drove along the glen—down by the *Northesk* (the *Ey* and *Mark* meeting become the *Northesk*), passing to the right another very pretty glen—*Glen Effach*, much wooded, and the whole landscape beautifully lit up. Before us all was light and bright, and behind the mist and rain seemed to come down heavily over the mountains.

Further on, we passed *Poul Skeinnie Bridge* and *Tarf Bridge*, both regular steep Highland bridges. To the right of the latter there is a new Free Kirk—further on *Captain Wemyss's Retreat*, a strange-looking place,—to the left *Mill Dane*—and, on a small eminence, the *Castle of Auch Mill*, which now resembles an old farm-house, but has traces of a terrace garden remaining. The hills round it and near the road to the left were like small mounds. A little further on again we came to a wood, where we got out and walked along *Major McInroy's Burn*. The path winds along through the wood just above this most curious narrow gorge, which is unlike any of the other lynns; the rocks are very peculiar, and the burn very narrow, with deep pools completely overhung by wood. It extends some way. The woods and grounds might be in *Wales*, or even in *Hawthornden*. We walked through the wood and a little way along the road, till the carriages overtook us. We had three miles further to drive to *Fettercairn*, in all 40 miles from *Balmoral*. We came upon a flat country, evidently much cultivated, but it was too dark to see anything.

At a quarter-past seven o'clock we reached the small quiet town, or rather village, of *Fettercairn*, for it was very small—not a creature stirring, and we got out at the quiet little inn, "Ramsay Arms," quite unobserved, and went at once upstairs. There was a very nice drawing-room, and next to it, a dining-room, both very clean and tidy—then to the left our bed-room, which was excessively small, but also very clean and neat, and much better furnished than at *Grantown*. Alice had a nice room, the same size as ours; then came a mere morsel of one, (with a "press bed,") in which Albert dressed; and then came Lady

Churchill's bed-room just beyond. Louis and
General Grey had rooms in an hotel, called "The
Temperance Hotel," opposite. We dined at eight,
a very nice, clean, good dinner. Grant and Brown
waited. They were rather nervous, but General
Grey and Lady Churchill carved, and they had
only to change the plates, which Brown soon got
into the way of doing. A little girl of the house
came in to help—but Grant turned her round to
prevent her looking at us! The landlord and landlady knew who we were, but *no one else* except the
coachman, and they kept the secret admirably.

The evening being bright and moonlight and
very still, we all went out, and walked through
the whole village, where not a creature moved ;—
through the principal little square, in the middle of
which was a sort of pillar or Town Cross on steps,
and Louis read, by the light of the moon, a proclama-
tion for collections of charities which was stuck on
it. We walked on along a lane a short way, hearing
nothing whatever—not a leaf moving—but the distant barking of a dog! Suddenly we heard a drum
and fifes! We were greatly alarmed, fearing we
had been recognized ; but Louis and General Grey,
who went back, saw nothing whatever. Still, as

we walked slowly back, we heard the noise from
time to time,—and when we reached the inn door
we stopped, and saw six men march up with fifes
and a drum (not a creature taking any notice of
them), go down the street, and back again. Grant
and Brown were out; but had no idea what it could
be. Albert asked the little maid, and the answer
was, "It's just a band," and that it walked about
in this way twice a week. How odd! It went
on playing some time after we got home. We
sat till half-past ten working, and Albert reading,
—and then retired to rest.

Saturday, September 21.

Got to sleep after two or three o'clock. The
morning was dull and close, and misty with a little
rain; hardly any one stirring; but a few people at
their work. A traveller had arrived at night, and
wanted to come up into the dining-room, which is
the "commercial travellers' room;" and they had
difficulty in telling him he could *not* stop there.
He joined Grant and Brown at their tea, and on his
asking, "What's the matter here?" Grant answered,

" It's a wedding party from *Aberdeen*." At " The
Temperance Hotel " they were very anxious to
know whom they had got. All, except General
Grey, breakfasted a little before nine. Brown acted
as my servant, brushing my skirt and boots, and
taking any message, and Grant as Albert's valet.

At a quarter to ten we started the same way as
before, except that we were in the carriage which
Lady Churchill and the General had yesterday.
It was unfortunately misty, and we could see no
distance. The people had just discovered who we
were, and a few cheered us as we went along. We
passed close to *Fettercairn*, Sir J. Forbes's house ;
then further on to the left, *Fasque*, belonging to Sir
T. Gladstone, who has evidently done a great deal
for the country, having built many good cottages.
We then came to a very long hill, at least four miles
in length, called the *Cairnie Month*, whence there is
a very fine view ; but which was entirely obscured
by a heavy driving mist. We walked up part of it,
and then for a little while Alice and I sat alone in
the carriage. We next came to the *Spittal Bridge*,
a curious high bridge with the *Dye Water* to the
left, and the *Spittal Burn* to the right. Sir T.
Gladstone's shooting-place is close to the *Bridge*

of Dye—where we changed carriages again, re-entering the double dog-cart—Albert and I inside, and Louis sitting behind. We went up a hill again and saw *Mount Battock* to the north-west, close to Sir T. Gladstone's shooting-lodge. You then come to an open country, with an extensive view towards *Aberdeen*, and to a very deep, rough ford, where you pass the *Feugh*, at a place called *White Stones*. It is very pretty and a fine glen with wood. About two miles further to the north-west, on the left, is *Finzean ;* and, a little beyond, is "King Durdun's Stone," as they call it, by the roadside — a large, heavy, ancient stone,— the history of which, however, we have not yet discovered. Then we passed *Mary's Well*, to the left of which is *Ballogie House*, a fine property belonging to Mr. Dyce Nicol. The harvest and everything seemed prosperous, and the country was very pretty. We got out at a very small village, (where the horses had some water, for it was a terribly long stage,) and walked a little way along the road. Alice, Lady Churchill, and I, went into the house of a tailor, which was very tidy, and the woman in it most friendly, asking us to rest there ; but not dreaming who we were.

We drove on again, watching ominous-looking clouds, which, however, cleared off afterwards. We saw the woods of Lord Huntly's forest, and the hills which one sees from the road to *Aboyne*. Instead of going on to *Aboyne* we turned to the left, leaving the *Bridge of Aboyne* (which we had not seen before) to the right. A little beyond this, out of sight of all habitations, we found the postmaster, with another carriage for us. This was 22 miles from *Fettercairn*. We crossed the *Tanar Water*, and drove to the left up *Glen Tanar*—a really beautiful and richly-wooded glen, between high hills—part of Lord Huntly's forest. We drove on about six miles, and then stopped, as it was past two, to get our luncheon. The day kept quite fair in spite of threatening clouds and gathering mist. The spot where we lunched was very pretty. This over, we walked on a little, and then got into the carriages again, and drove to the end of the glen—out of the trees to *Eatnoch*, on to a keeper's house in the glen —a very lonely place, where our ponies were. It was about four when we arrived. A wretched idiot girl was here by herself, as tall as Lady Churchill ; but a good deal bent, and dressed like a child, with a pinafore and short-cut hair. She sat on the ground with her hands round her knees, rocking herself to and fro and laughing; she then got up and walked towards us. General Grey put himself before me, and she went up to him, and began taking hold of his coat, and putting her hand into his pockets, which set us all off laughing, sad as it was. An old man walked up hastily soon after, and on Lady Churchill asking him if he knew that poor girl, he said, " Yes, she belongs to me, she has a weakness in her mind ; " and led her off hurriedly.

We walked on a few hundred yards, and then mounted our ponies a little higher up, and then proceeded across the other shoulder of the hill we had come down yesterday—crossed the boggy part, and came over the *Polach* just as in going. The mist on the distant hills, *Mount Keen*, &c., made it feel chilly. Coming down the peat-road * to the *Bridge of Muich*, the view of the

* Grant told me in May, 1862, that, when the Prince stopped behind with him, looking at the Choils which he intended as a deer-forest for the Prince of Wales, and giving his directions as to the planting in Glen Muich, he said to Grant, —" You and I may be dead and gone before that." In less than three months, alas! his words were verified as regards himself ! He was ever cheerful, but ever ready and prepared.

valleys of *Muich*, *Gairn*, and *Ballater* was beautiful. As we went along I talked frequently with good Grant.

We found my dearest Mother's sociable, a fine large one, which she has left to Albert, waiting to take us back. It made me very sad, and filled my eyes with tears. Oh, in the midst of cheerfulness, I feel so sad! But being out a great deal here—and seeing new and fine scenery, does me good.

We got back to *Balmoral*, much pleased with our expedition, at seven o'clock. We had gone 42 miles to-day, and 40 yesterday, in all 82.

EXPEDITION TO LOCH AVON.

Saturday, September 28, 1861.

Looked out very anxiously. A doubtful morning; still gleams of sunshine burst through the mist, and it seemed improving all round. We breakfasted at a quarter to eight, with Alice and Louis, in our sitting-room; and started at half-past eight. Louis and Alice with us, Grant and Brown on the box, as usual. The morning greatly improved.

We drove along the north side of the river, the day clearing very much, and becoming really fine. We took post-horses at *Castleton*, and drove up to the *Derry* (the road up *Glen Luie* very bad indeed); and here we mounted our ponies, and proceeded the usual way up *Glen Derry*, as far as where the path turns up to *Loch Etchan*. Instead of going that way, we proceeded straight on — a dreadfully rough, stony road, though not steep, but rougher than anything we ever rode upon before, and terrible for the poor horses' feet. We passed by two little lakes called the *Dhoolochans*, opposite to where the glen runs down to *Inchrory*, and after crossing them, there was a short boggy bit, where I got off and walked some way on the opposite side, along the "brae" of the hill, on the other side of which the loch lies, and then got on again. It was so saturated with water, that the moss and grass and everything were soaked,—not very pleasant riding, particularly as it was along the slope of the hill. We went on and on, nearly two miles from the foot of this hill, expecting to see the loch, but another low hill hid it from us, till at length we came in sight of it; and nothing could be grander and wilder—the rocks are so grand and precipitous, and the snow on *Ben Muich Dhui* had such a fine effect.

We saw the spot at the foot of *Loch Etchan* to which we scrambled last year, and looked down upon *Loch Avon*. It was very cold and windy. At length, at a quarter-past two, we sat down behind a large stone a little above the loch (unfortunately, we could not go to the extreme

end, where the water rushes into it). We lunched
as quickly as we could, and then began walking
back, and crossed the hill higher up than in
coming. I walked for some time, but it was not
easy, from the great wet and the very uneven
ground. Good Louis helped me often; Albert
and Alice running along without assistance.
Remounted my pony, which, as well as Albert's,
went beautifully, carefully led by that most attentive of servants, Brown. I had again to get off
before we crossed by the *Dhoolochans;* but after
that we rode back the whole way.

We had the same guide, Charlie Stewart, who
took us to *Glen Fishie* last year, and who walks
wonderfully. We had two slight showers going
down, and saw that there had been much more
rain below. We found the *Ford of the Derry*
very deep, nearly up to the ponies' girths; and
the roughness and stoniness of the road is beyond
everything, but the ponies picked their way like
cats. We were down at the *Derry* by nearly six
o'clock; the distance to *Loch Avon* being ten
miles. Found our carriages there : it was already
getting darkish, but still it was quite light enough
to enable the post-boys to see their way.

At the bridge at *Mar Lodge*, Brown lit the lanterns. We gave him and Grant our plaids to put on, as we always do when they have walked a long way with us and drive afterwards. We took our own horses at *Castleton*, and reached *Balmoral* at ten minutes past eight, much pleased with the success of our expedition, and really *not* tired. We dined *en famille*.

Third Great Expedition :—To Glen Fishie, Dalwhinnie, and Blair Athole.

Tuesday, October 8, 1861.

The morning was dull and rather overcast; however, we decided to go. General Grey had gone on before. We three ladies drove in the sociable : Albert and Louis in a carriage from *Castleton.* The clouds looked heavy and dark, though not like mist hanging on the mountains. Down came a heavy shower; but before we reached *Castleton* it cleared; blue sky appeared; and, as there was much wind, Grant thought all would be well, and the day very fine. Changed horses at *Castleton,* and drove beyond the *Linn of Dee* to the *Giuly* or *Geldie Water*—just where last year we mounted our ponies, 18 miles from *Balmoral.* Here we found our ponies—" Inchrory " for me, and a new pony for Alice—a tall grey

one, ugly but safe. The others rode their usual
ones. The same guide, Charlie Stewart, was
there, and a pony for the luncheon panniers,
and a spare one for Grant and others to ride in
turn.

We started about ten minutes past eleven,
and proceeded exactly as last year, fording the
Geidie at first very frequently. The ground
was wet, but not worse than last year. We
had gone on very well for about an hour, when
the mist thickened all round, and down came
heavy, or at least beating, rain with wind.
With the help of an umbrella, and water-
proofs and a plaid, I kept quite dry. Dearest
Albert, who walked from the time the ground
became boggy, got very wet, but was none the
worse for it, and we got through it much better
than before ; we ladies never having to get
off our ponies. At length at two o'clock, just
as we were entering that beautiful *Glen Fishie*,
which at its commencement reminds one of
Mc Inroy's Burn, it cleared, and became quite
fine and very mild. Brown waded through the
Etchart leading my pony; and then two of the
others, who were riding together on another pony,

dropped the whole bundle of cloaks into the water!

The falls of the *Stron-na-Barin*, with that narrow steep glen, which you ride up, crossing at the bottom, were in great beauty. We stopped before we enterèd the wood, and lunched on the bank overhanging the river, where General Grey joined us, and gave us an account of his arrangements. We lunched rather hurriedly, remounted our ponies and rode a short way— till we came near to a very steep place, not very pleasant to ride. So fine! numberless little burns running down in cascades. We walked a short way, and then remounted our ponies; but as we were to keep on the other side of the river, not by the *Invereshie* huts, we had to get off for a few hundred yards, the path being so narrow as to make it utterly unsafe to ride. Alice's pony already began to slip. The huts, surrounded by magnificent fir-trees, and by quantities of juniper-bushes, looked lovelier than ever; and we gazed with sorrow at their utter ruin. I felt what a delightful little encampment it must have been, and how enchanting to live in such a spot as this beautiful solitary wood in a glen surrounded by the high hills. We got off, and went into one of the huts to look at a fresco of stags of Landseer's, over a chimney-piece. Grant, on a pony, led me through the *Fishie* (all the fords are deep) at the foot of the farm - houses, where we met Lord and Lady Alexander Russell last year—and where we this time found two carriages. We dismounted and entered them, and were off at five o'clock—we were to have started at four.

We four drove together by the same way as we rode last year (and nothing could be rougher for driving), quite to the second wood, which led us past *Loch Inch*; but we turned short of the loch to the left along the high road. Unfortunately by this time it was nearly dark, and we therefore lost a great deal of the fine scenery. We had ridden 15 miles. We drove along the road over several bridges—the *Bridge of Carr*, close below the ruined *Castle of Ruthven*, which we could just descry in the dusk—and on a long wooden bridge over the *Spey* to an inn at *Kingussie*, a very straggling place with very few cottages. Already, before we arrived there, we were struck by people standing at their cottage doors, and evidently looking out, which made us believe we were expected. At *Kingussie* there was a small, curious, chattering crowd of people—who, how-ever, did not really make us out, but evidently suspected who we were. Grant and Brown kept them off the carriages, and gave them evasive answers, directing them to the wrong carriage, which was most amusing. One old gentleman, with a high wide-awake, was especially inquisitive.

We started again, and went on and on, passing through the village of *Newtonmoore*, where the footman Mc Donald* comes from. Here the *Spey* is crossed at its junction with the *Truim*, and then the road ascends for ten miles more to *Dalwhinnie*. It became cold and windy with occasional rain. At length, and not till a quarter to nine, we reached the inn of *Dalwhinnie*,—29 miles from where we had left our ponies,—which stands by itself, away from any village. Here, again, there were a few people assembled, and I thought they knew us; but it seems they did not, and it was only when we arrived that one

* He died at Abergeldie last year of consumption ; and his widow, an excellent person, daughter of Mitchell the black-smith at Balmoral, is now my wardrobe-maid.

of the maids recognized me. She had seen me at *Aberdeen* and *Edinburgh*. We went upstairs: the inn was much larger than at *Fettercairn*, but not nearly so nice and cheerful; there was a drawing-room and a dining-room; and we had a very good-sized bedroom. Albert had a dressing-room of equal size. Mary Andrews* (who was very useful and efficient) and Lady Churchill's maid had a room together, every one being in the house; but unfortunately there was hardly anything to eat, and there was only tea, and two miserable starved Highland chickens, without any potatoes! No pudding, and no *fun;* no little maid (the two there not wishing to come in), nor our two people—who were wet and drying our and their things—to wait on us! It was not a nice supper; and the evening was wet. As it was late we soon retired to rest. Mary and Maxted (Lady Churchill's maid) had been dining below with Grant, Brown, and Stewart (who came, the same as last time, with the maids) in the " commercial room" at the foot of the stairs. They had only the remnants of our two starved chickens!

* One of my wardrobe-maids—now dresser to Princess Helena (Princess Christian). Her father was thirty-eight years with my dear uncle the King of the Belgians.

Wednesday, October 9.

A bright morning, which was very charming. Albert found, on getting up, that Cluny Macpherson, with his piper and two ladies, had arrived quite early in the morning; and, while we were dressing, we heard a drum and fife—and discovered that the newly-formed volunteers had arrived—all indicating that we were discovered. However, there was scarcely any population, and it did not signify. The fat old landlady had put on a black satin dress, with white ribbons and orange flowers! We had breakfast at a quarter to nine o'clock; at half-past nine we started. Cluny was at the door with his wife and daughters with nosegays, and the volunteers were drawn up in front of the inn. They had all assembled since Saturday afternoon!

We drove as we did yesterday. Fine and very wild scenery, high wild hills, and no habitations. We went by the *Pass of Drumouchter*, with fine hills on both sides and in front of us; passed between two, the one on our left called *The Boar of Badenoch*, and that on the right, *The*

Athole Sow. The *Pass of Drumouchter* separates *Perthshire* from *Inverness-shire.*

Again, a little farther on, we came to *Loch Garry*, which is very beautiful—but the mist covered the furthest hills, and the extreme distance was clouded. There is a small shooting-lodge, or farm, charmingly situated, looking up the glen on both sides, and with the loch in front; we did not hear to whom it belonged. We passed many drovers, without their herds and flocks, returning, Grant told us, from *Falkirk*. We had one very heavy shower after *Loch Garry* and before we came to *Dalnacardoch Inn*, 13 miles from *Dalwhinnie*. The road goes beside the *Garry*. The country for a time became flatter; but was a good deal cultivated. At *Dalnacardoch Inn* there was a suspicion and expectation of our arrival. Four horses with smart postilions were in waiting; but, on General Grey's saying that this was *not* the party, but the one for whom only two horses had been ordered, a shabby pair of horses were put in ; a shabby driver driving from the box (as throughout this journey), and off we started.

The *Garry* is very fine, rolling along over large stones—like the *Quoich* and the *Fishie*, and forming perpetual falls, with birch and mountain-ash growing down to the water's edge. We had some more heavy showers. A few miles from *Dalnacardoch* the Duke of Athole (in his kilt and shooting-jacket, as usual) met us on a pretty little chestnut pony, and rode the whole time near the carriage. He said, there were vague suspicions and rumours of our coming, but he had told no one anything. There was again a shower, but it cleared when we came in sight of *Ben-y-Ghlo*, and the splendid *Pass of Killiekrankie*, which, with the birch all golden,—not, as on *Dee-side*, bereft of leaves,—looked very beautiful.

We passed by the *Bruar*, and the road to the *Falls of the Bruar*, but could not stop. The Duke took us through a new approach, which is extremely pretty; but near which, I cannot help regretting, the railroad will come, as well as along the road by which we drove through the *Pass of Drumouchter*. The Duke has made great improvements, and the path looked beautiful, surrounded as it is by hills; and the foliage still full, though in all its autumn tints—the whole being lit up with bright sunshine. We drove through an avenue, and in a few minutes more were at the door of the old castle. A thousand recollections of seventeen years ago crowded upon me—all seemed so familiar again! No one there except the dear Duchess, who stood at the door, and whom I warmly embraced; and Miss Mac Gregor. How well I recognized the hall with all the sporting trophies; and the staircase, which we went up at once. The Duchess took us to a room which I recognized immediately as the one where Lady Canning lived. There we took off our things— then went to look at the old and really very hand- some rooms in which we had lived—the one in which Vicky had slept in two chairs, then not four years old! In the dining-room we took some coffee, which was most welcome; and then we looked at all the stags' horns put up in one of the corridors below; saw the Duke's pet dog, a smooth-haired black terrier, very fat; and then got into the carriage, a very peculiar one, viz., a *boat*—a mere boat (which is very light), put on four wheels, drawn by a pair of horses with a postilion. Into this we four got, with the Duke and Duchess and the dog;—Lady Churchill, General Grey, and Miss Mac Gregor going in another carriage; with our two servants on the box, to whom all this was quite new and a great treat. The morning was beautiful. It was half-past twelve—we drove up by the avenue and about a favourite walk of ours in '44, passed through the gate, and came on to *Glen Tilt*—which is most striking, the road winding along, first on one side of the *Tilt*, and then on the other; the fine high hills rising very abruptly from each side of the rapid, rocky, stony river *Tilt*—the trees, chiefly birch and alder, overhanging the water.

We passed the *Marble Lodge*, in which one of the keepers lives, and came to *Forest Lodge*, where the road for carriages ends, and the glen widens. There were our ponies, which had passed the night at the *Bainoch* or *Beynoch* (a shooting "shiel" of Lord Fife's). They came over this morning; but, poor beasts, without having had any corn! *Forest Lodge* is eight miles from *Blair*. There we took leave of the dear Duchess; and saw old Peter Frazer, the former head-keeper there, now walking with the aid of two sticks! The Duke's keepers were there, his pipers, and a gentleman staying on a visit with him.

It was barely two o'clock when we started. We on our ponies, the Duke and his men (twelve altogether) on foot—Sandy Mc Ara, now head-keeper, grown old and grey, and two pipers, preceded us; the two latter playing alternately the whole time, which had a most cheerful effect. The wild strains sounded so softly amid those noble hills; and our caravan winding along—our people and the Duke's all in kilts, and the ponies, made altogether a most picturesque scene.

One of the Duke's keepers, Donald Macbeath, is a guardsman, and was in the *Crimea*. He is a celebrated marksman, and a fine-looking man, as all the Duke's men are. For some little time it was easy riding, but soon we came to a rougher path, more on the "brae" of the hill, where the pony required to be led, which I always have done, either when it is at all rough or bad, or when the pony has to be got on faster.

The Duke walked near me the greater part of the time; amusingly saying, in reference to former times, that he did not offer to lead me, as he knew I had no confidence in him. I replied, laughingly, "Oh, no, only I like best being led by the person I am accustomed to."

At length, at about three, we stopped, and lunched at a place called *Dalcronachie*, looking up a glen towards *Loch Loch*—on a high bank overhanging the *Tilt*. Looking back the view was very fine; so, while the things were being unpacked for lunch, we sketched. We brought our own luncheon, and the remainder was as usual given to the men, but this time there were a great many to feed. After luncheon, we set off again. I walked a few paces; but as it was very wet, and the road very rough, by Albert's desire I got on again. A very few minutes brought us to the celebrated ford of the *Tarff*, (*Poll Tarff* it is called,) which is very deep—and after heavy rain almost impassable. The Duke offered to lead the pony on one side, and talked of Sandy for the other side, but I asked for Brown (whom I have far the most confidence in) to lead the pony, the Duke taking hold of it (as he did frequently) on the other side. Sandy Mc Ara, the guide, and the two pipers went first, playing all the time. To all appearance the ford of the *Tarff* was not deeper than the other fords, but once in it the men were above their knees—and suddenly in the middle, where the current, from the fine, high, full falls, is very strong, it was nearly up to the men's waists. Here Sandy returned, and I said to the Duke (which he afterwards joked with Sandy about) that I thought he (Sandy) had better take the Duke's place; he did so, and we came very well through, all the others following, the men chiefly wading—Albert (close behind me) and the others riding through—and some of our people coming over double on the ponies. General Grey had little Peter Robertson up behind him.

The road after this became almost precipitous, and indeed made riding very unpleasant; but being wet, and difficult to walk, we ladies rode, Albert walking the greater part of the time. Only once, for a very few steps, I had to get off, as the pony could hardly keep its footing. As it was, Brown constantly could not walk next to the pony, but had to scramble below, or pull it after him. The Duke was indefatigable.

The *Tilt* becomes narrower and narrower, till its first source is almost invisible. The *Tarff* flows into the *Tilt*, about two miles or more beyond the falls. We emerged from the pass upon an open valley—with less high hills and with the hills of *Braemar* before us. We crossed the *Bainoch* or *Bynack*, quite a small stream, and when we came to the " County March "—where *Perth* and *Aberdeen*

join—we halted. The Duke gave Albert and me
some whisky to drink, out of an old silver flask
of his own, and then made a short speech proposing
my health, expressing the pleasure with which
he and all had received me at *Blair*, and hoping
that I would return as often as I liked, and that I
should have a safe return home ; ending by the
true Highland " Nis ! nis ! nis ! Sit air a-nis !
" A-ris ! a-ris ! a-ris ! " (pronounced : " Neesh !
" neesh ! neesh ! Sheet eir, a-neesh ! A-rees ! a-rees !
" a-rees !") which means : " Now ! now ! now ! That
" to him, now ! Again ! again ! again ! " which was
responded to by cheering from all. Grant then proposed "three cheers for the Duke of Athole," which
was also very warmly responded to;—my pony
(good " Inchrory "), which went admirably, rather
resenting the vehemence of Brown's cheering.

We then went on again for about three miles
to the *Bainoch*, which we reached at ten minutes
to six, when it was already nearly dark. As we
approached the "shiel," the pipers struck up, and
played. The ponies went so well with the pipes, and
altogether it was very pleasant to ride and walk
with them. They played " the Athole Highlanders " when we started, and again in coming in.

Lady Fife had very kindly come down to the *Bainoch* herself, where she gave us tea, which was very welcome. We then got into our carriages, wishing the good Duke of Athole good-by. He was going back the whole way—which was certainly rather a hazardous proceeding, at least an adventurous one, considering the night, and that there was no moon—and what the road was! We got home safely at a quarter-past eight. The night was quite warm, though slightly showery —but became very clear and starlight later.

We had travelled 69 miles to-day, and 60 yesterday. This was the pleasantest and most enjoyable expedition I *ever* made; and the recollection of it will always be most agreeable to me, and increase my wish to make more! Was so glad dear Louis (who is a charming companion) was with us. Have enjoyed nothing as much, or indeed felt so much cheered by anything, since my great sorrow. * Did not feel tired. We ladies did not dress, and dined *en famille;* looking at maps of the *Highlands* after dinner.

* The death of the Duchess of Kent.

Last Expedition.

Wednesday, October 16, 1861.

To our great satisfaction it was a most beautiful morning. Not a cloud was on the bright blue sky, and it was perfectly calm. There had been a sharp frost which lay on parts of the grass, and the mountains were beautifully lit up, with those very blue shades upon them, like the bloom on a plum. Up early, and breakfasted with Alice, Louis, and Lenchen, in our room. At twenty minutes to nine o'clock we started, with Alice, Lenchen, and Louis. The morning was beyond everything splendid, and the country in such beauty, though the poor trees are nearly leafless.

Near *Castleton*, and indeed all along the road, in the shade, the frost still lay, and the air was very sharp. We took post-horses at *Castleton*, and proceeded up *Glen Clunie* to *Glen Callater*, which looked lovely, and which Albert admired much. In a little more than two hours we were at *Loch Callater*—the road was very bad indeed as we approached the loch, where our ponies were waiting for us. After walking a few paces we remounted them, I on my good " Fyvie," and Alice on " Inchrory."

The day was glorious—and the whole expedition delightful, and very easily performed. We ascended *Little Cairn Turc*, on the north side of *Loch Callater*, up a sort of footpath very easy and even, upon ground that was almost flat, rising very gradually, but imperceptibly; and the view became wonderfully extensive. The top of *Cairn Turc* is quite flat—with moss and grass— so that you could drive upon it. It is very high, for you see the high table-land behind the highest point of *Loch-na-Gar*. On that side you have no view; but from the other it is wonderfully extensive. It was so clear and bright, and so still there, reminding us of the day on *Ben Muich Dhui* last year.

There rose immediately behind us *Ben Muich Dhui*, which you hardly ever see, and the shape of which is not fine, with its surrounding mountains of *Cairngorm, Brae Riach, Ben Avon* or *A'an, Ben-na-Bhourd,* &c. We saw *Ben-y-Ghlo* quite clearly, and all that range of hills; then, further west, *Shichallion,* near *Loch Tay;* the mountains which are near the *Black Mount;* and, quite on the horizon, we could discern *Ben Nevis,* which is above *Fort William.*

Going up *Cairn Turc* we looked down upon *Loch Canter,* a small loch above *Loch Callater,* very wild and dark. We proceeded to *Cairn Glaishie,* at the extreme point of which a cairn has been erected. We got off to take a look at the wonderful panorama which lay stretched out before us. We looked on *Fifeshire,* and the country between *Perth* and *Stirling,* the *Lomond Hills,* &c. It was beautifully clear, and really it was most interesting to look over such an immense extent of the *Highlands.* I give a very poor description of it ; but here follows a rough account of the places we saw :—

To the North—*Ben Muich Dhui, Brae Riach, Cairngorm, Ben Avon, Ben-na-Bhourd.*

To the East—*Loch-na-Gar,* &c.

To the South-West—*Ben-y-Ghlo* or *Ben-y-Gloe,* and the surrounding hills beyond *Shichallion,* and

the mountains between *Dunkeld* and the *Black
Mount.*

Quite in the extreme West—*Ben Nevis.*

To the South—the *Lomond Hills; Perth* in the
middle distance.

We walked on a little way, and then I got upon
my pony. Another half hour's riding again over
such singular flat table-land, brought us on to the
edge of the valley of *Cairn Lochan,* which is indeed
" a bonnie place." It reminded me and Louis of
Clova; only there one did not see the immense
extent of mountains behind. *Cairn Lochan* is a
narrow valley, the river *Isla* winding through
it like a silver ribbon, with trees at the bottom.
The hills are green and steep, but towards the
head of the valley there are fine precipices. We
had then to take a somewhat circuitous route in
order to avoid some bogs, and to come to a spot
where we looked right up the valley for an immense distance; to the left, or rather more to the
south, was *Glen Isla,* another glen, but wider, and
not with the same high mountains as *Cairn
Lochan.* Beyond *Glen Isla* were seen the *Lomond
Hills* behind *Kinross,* at the foot of which is *Loch
Leven.*

We sat on a very precipitous place, which made one dread any one's moving backwards; and here, at a little before two o'clock, we lunched. The lights were charmingly soft, and, as I said before, like the bloom on a plum. The luncheon was very acceptable, for the air was extremely keen, and we found ice thicker than a shilling on the top of *Cairn Turc*, which did not melt when Brown took it and kept it in his hand.

Helena was so delighted, for this was *the only really great* expedition in which she had accompanied us.

Duncan and the keeper at *Loch Callater* (R. Stewart) went with us as guides.

I made some hasty sketches; and then Albert wrote on a bit of paper that we had lunched here, put it into the Selters-water bottle, and buried it there, or rather stuck it into the ground. Grant had done the same when we visited *Ben Muich Dhui* the first time. This over, we walked part of the way back which we had ridden to avoid the bogs,—we ladies walking only a short way, and then riding. We altered our course, and left *Cairn Glaishie* to our right, and went in the direction of the *Cairn Wall*. Looking back on the distant hills above *Glen Isla* and *Cairn Lochan* (Lord Airlie's " Country "), it was even more beautiful; for, as the day advanced, the mountains became clearer, and clearer, of a lovely blue, while the valleys were in shadow. *Shichallion*, and those further ranges, were also most perfectly to be seen, and gave me such a longing for further Highland expeditions! We went over *Garbchory*, looking down on the road to the *Spittal;* and on the lower mountains, which are most curiously connected one with another, and which, from the height we were, we could look down upon.

Here follows the account of our route, with all the names as written down by Duncan. I cannot " mind " the names, as they say here.

From *Balmoral* to—
Loch Callater, four miles,
Left *Loch Callater* at 11 o'clock, A.M.,
Little Cairn Turc,
Big Cairn Turc,
Loch Canter,
Cairn Glaishie,
Cairn Lochan,
Ca-Ness, six miles.

Returning route :—
Cairn Lochan,
Cairn Glashie,
Garb Chory,
Month Eigie Road,
Glass Meall,
Fian Chory,
Aron Ghey,
Shean Spittal Bridge, 4.30 P.M.,
Shean Spittal Bridge to *Balmoral,* 16 miles.

This gave one a very good idea of the geography of the country, which delighted dear Albert, as this expedition was quite in a different direction from any that we had ever made before. But my head is so very ungeographical, that I cannot describe it. We came down by the *Month Eigie,* a steep hill covered with grass—down part of which I rode, walking where it was steepest; but it was so wet and slippery that I had two falls. We got down to the road to the *Spittal Bridge,* about 15 miles from *Castleton,* at nearly half-past four, and then down along the new road, at least that part of it which is finished, and which is to extend to the *Cairn Wall.* We went back on our side of the river ; and if we had been a little earlier, Albert might have got a stag—but it was too late.   The moon rose and shone most beautifully, and we returned at twenty minutes to seven o'clock, much pleased and interested with this delightful expedition.   Alas ! I fear our *last* great one !

(IT WAS OUR LAST ONE !—1867.)

TOURS

in

ENGLAND AND IRELAND,

and

YACHTING EXCURSIONS.

FIRST VISIT TO IRELAND.

On Board the Victoria and Albert,
in the Cove of Cork,
Thursday, August 2, 1849.

ARRIVED here after a quick but not very pleasant passage. The day was fine and bright, and the sea to all appearance very smooth ; but there was a dreadful swell, which made one incapable of reading or doing anything. We passed the *Land's End* at nine o'clock in the morning. When we went on deck after eight in the evening, we were close to the *Cove of Cork*, and could see many bonfires on the hill, and the rockets and lights that were sent off from the different steamers. The harbour is immense, though the land is not very high, and entering by twilight it had a very fine effect. Lady Jocelyn, Miss Dawson, Lord Fortescue (Lord Steward), Sir George Grey (Secretary of State for the Home Department), Miss Hildyard, Sir James Clark, and Mr. Birch are on board with us. The equerries, Colonel Phipps and Colonel Gordon, are on board the " Black Eagle."

Friday, August 3.

The day was grey and excessively " muggy," which is the character of the Irish climate. The ships saluted at eight o'clock, and the " Ganges " (the flag-ship and a three-decker) and the " Hogue" (a three-decker cut down, with very heavy guns, and with a screw put into her), which are both very near us, made a great noise. The harbour is very extensive, and there are several islands in it, one of which is very large. *Spike Island* is immediately opposite us, and has a convict prison ; near it another island with the depôt, &c. In a line with that is the town of *Cove*, picturesquely built up a hill. The two war-steamers have only just come in. The Admiral (Dixon) and the Captains of the vessels came on board. Later, Lord Bandon (Lord-Lieutenant of the county), Lord Thomond, General Turner, Commander of the Forces at Cork, presented their respects, and

Albert went on shore, and I occupied myself in writing and sketching. Albert returned before our luncheon, and had been walking about and visiting some of the cabins.

We left the yacht at two with the ladies and gentlemen, and went on board the " Fairy," which was surrounded with rowing and sailing boats. We first went round the harbour, all the ships saluting, as well as numbers of steamers and yachts. We then went in to *Cove* and lay alongside the landing-place, which was very prettily decorated; and covered with people; and yachts, ships and boats crowding all round. The two Members, Messrs. Roche and Power, as well as other gentlemen, including the Roman Catholic and Protestant clergymen, and then the members of the Yacht Club, presented addresses. After which, to give the people the satisfaction of calling the place *Queenstown,* in honour of its being the first spot on which I set foot upon Irish ground, I stepped on shore amidst the roar of cannon (for the artillery were placed so close as quite to shake the temporary room which we entered); and the enthusiastic shouts of the people. We immediately re-embarked and proceeded up the river *Lee* towards *Cork*. It is extremely pretty and richly wooded, and reminded me of the *Tamar*. The first feature of interest we passed was a little bathing-place, called *Monkstown*, and later *Blackrock Castle*, at which point we stopped to receive a salmon, and a very pretty address from the poor fishermen of *Blackrock*.

As we approached the city we saw people streaming in, on foot, on horseback, and many in jaunting-cars. When we reached *Cork* the " Fairy " again lay alongside, and we received all the addresses : first, from the Mayor and Corporation (I knighted the Mayor immediately afterwards), then from the Protestant Bishop and clergy; from the Roman Catholic Bishop and clergy; from the Lord-Lieutenant of the county, the Sheriffs, and others. The two Judges, who were holding their courts, also came on board in their robes. After all this was over we landed, and walked some few paces on to where Lord Bandon's carriage was ready to receive us. The ladies went with us, and Lord Bandon and the General rode on each side of the carriage. The Mayor preceded us, and many (Lord Listowel among the number,) followed on horseback or in carriages. The 12th

Lancers escorted us, and the Pensioners and Infantry lined the streets.

I cannot describe our route, but it will suffice to say that it took two hours ; that we drove through the principal streets ; twice through some of them ; that they were densely crowded, decorated with flowers and triumphal arches ; that the heat and dust were great ; that we passed by the new College which is building—one of the four which are ordered by Act of Parliament ; that our reception was most enthusiastic ; and that everything went off to perfection, and was very well arranged. *Cork* is not at all like an English town, and looks rather foreign. The crowd is a noisy, excitable, but very good-humoured one, running and pushing about, and laughing, talking, and shrieking. The beauty of the women is very remarkable, and struck us much ; such beautiful dark eyes and hair, and such fine teeth ; almost every third woman was pretty, and some remarkably so. They wear no bonnets, and generally long blue cloaks ; the men are very poorly, often raggedly dressed ; and many wear blue coats and short breeches with blue stockings.

We re-embarked at the same place and returned just as we came.

Kingstown Harbour, Dublin Bay,
Sunday, August 5.

Safely arrived here : I now continue my account. For the first two hours and a half the sea, though rough, was not disagreeable. We entered *Waterford Harbour* yesterday at twenty minutes to four o'clock. The harbour is rocky on the right as one enters, and very flat to the left; as one proceeds the land rises on either side. We passed a little fort called *Duncannon Fort,* whence James II. embarked after the battle of the *Boyne,* and from which they had not saluted for fifty years. Further up, between two little villages, one on either side, each with its little chapel, picturesquely situated on the top of the rock or hill, we anchored. The little fishing place to our left is called *Passage,* and is famous for salmon ; we had an excellent specimen for our dinner. Albert decided on going to *Waterford,* ten miles up the river, in the " Fairy," with the boys, but as I felt giddy and tired, I preferred remaining quietly on board sketching. Albert returned after seven o'clock ; he had not landed.

Viceregal Lodge, Phœnix Park,
Monday, August 6.

Here we are in this very pretty spot, with
a lovely view of the *Wicklow Hills* from the
window. But now to return to yesterday's pro-
ceedings. We got under weigh at half-past eight
o'clock; for three hours it was dreadfully rough,
and I and the poor children were very sea-sick.
When we had passed the *Tuscar Rock* in *Wexford*
the sea became smoother, and shortly after, quite
smooth, and the evening beautiful. After we
passed *Arklow Head*, the *Wicklow Hills* came in
sight—they are beautiful. The *Sugarloaf* and
Carrick Mountain have finely pointed outlines,
with low hills in front and much wood. At
half-past six we came in sight of *Dublin Bay*,
and were met by the " Sphynx" and " Stromboli"
(which had been sent on to wait and to come in
with us), the " Trident," and, quite close to the
harbour, by the "Dragon," another war-steamer.
With this large squadron we steamed slowly and
majestically into the harbour of *Kingstown*, which
was covered with thousands and thousands of

spectators, cheering most enthusiastically. It is a splendid harbour, and was full of ships of every kind. The wharf, where the landing-place was prepared, was densely crowded, and altogether it was a noble and stirring scene. It was just seven when we entered, and the setting sun lit up the country, the fine buildings, and the whole scene with a glowing light, which was truly beautiful. We were soon surrounded by boats, and the enthusiasm and excitement of the people were extreme.

While we were at breakfast the yacht was brought close up to the wharf, which was lined with troops. Lord and Lady Clarendon and George* came on board; also Lords Lansdowne and Clanricarde, the Primate, the Archbishop of Dublin, and many others. The address was presented by the Sheriff and gentlemen of the county. As the clock struck ten we disembarked, stepping on shore from the yacht, Albert leading me and the children, and all the others following us. An immense multitude had assembled, who cheered most enthusiastically, the ships saluting and the bands playing, and it was

* The Duke of Cambridge.

really very striking. The space we had to walk along to the railroad was covered in; and lined with ladies and gentlemen strewing flowers. We entered the railway-carriages with the children, the Clarendons, and the three ladies; and in a quarter of an hour reached the Dublin station. Here we found our carriages with the postilions in their Ascot liveries. The two eldest children went with us, and the two younger ones with the three ladies. Sir Edward Blakeney, Commander-in-Chief in Ireland, rode on one side of the carriage and George on the other, followed by a brilliant staff, and escorted by the 17th Lancers and the Carabiniers.

It was a wonderful and striking scene, such masses of human beings, so enthusiastic, so excited, yet such perfect order maintained; then the numbers of troops, the different bands stationed at certain distances, the waving of hats and handkerchiefs, the bursts of welcome which rent the air,—all made it a never-to-be-forgotten scene; when one reflected how lately the country had been in open revolt and under martial law.

Dublin is a very fine city; and *Sackville Street* and *Merrion Square* are remarkably large and

handsome ; and the *Bank, Trinity College*, &c. are
noble buildings. There are no gates to the town,
but temporary ones were erected under an arch ;
and here we stopped, and the Mayor presented
me the keys with some appropriate words. At
the last triumphal arch a poor little dove was let
down into my lap, with an olive branch round
its neck, alive and very tame. The heat and
dust were tremendous. We reached *Phœnix
Park*, which is very extensive, at twelve. Lord
and Lady Clarendon and all the household
received us at the door. It is a nice comfortable
house, reminding us of *Claremont*, with a pretty
terrace garden in front (laid out by Lady Nor-
manby), and has a very extensive view of the
Park and the fine range of the *Wicklow Mountains*. We are most comfortably lodged, and have
very nice rooms.

Tuesday, August 7.

We drove into *Dublin*—with our two ladies—
in Lord Clarendon's carriage, the gentlemen
following ; and without any escort. The people
were very enthusiastic, and cheered a great deal.

the Directors
ng-room, and
of Lords and
 was the old
drove to the
by the Arch-
Archbishop
an of eighty),
th the school.
nd the *Boys'*
oys was ex-
many very
wonderfully.
d, and their
ately, if the
g enforced is
and charity.
be the case
are educated
ed as school-
we visited

Trinity College, the Irish University, which is not
conducted upon so liberal a system, but into which
Roman Catholics are admitted. Dr. Todd, the
secretary, and a very learned man, well versed in

Sun Rises 7h. 45m. Sets 3h. 54m.
Moon: New M. 6. First Q. 13.

DECEMBER

3

MONDAY

Though I walk through the valley
of the shadow of death, I will fear
no evil; for Thou art with me.

Psalm 23. 4.

"PEACE! JOY!"

When preaching what proved to
be his last sermon, the Rev. H. L.
Lyte said: "Oh, brethren, I can
speak feelingly, experimentally, on
this point; and I stand here among
you seasonably to-day as alive
from the dead, if I may hope to
impress upon you, and induce you
to prepare for that solemn hour,
which must come to all, by a
timely acquaintance with, appre-
ciation of, dependence on, the
death of Christ!"

Later that evening, though very
weary, he wrote the great hymn,
"Abide with me, fast falls the
eventide," and two months later,
when he passed to his eternal rest,
his last words were: "Peace! Joy!"

Living above self and for God,
is real living for eternity.

Duncan Matheson.

the Irish language, showed us some most interesting ancient manuscripts and relics, including St. Columba's Book (in which we wrote our names), and the original harp of King O'Brian, supposed to be the one from which the Irish arms are taken. The library is a very large handsome room, like that in *Trinity College, Cambridge.* We then proceeded towards home, the crowd in the streets immense, and so loyal. It rained a little at intervals. Home by a little past one. Albert went into *Dublin* again after luncheon, and I wrote and read, and heard our children say some lessons.

At five we proceeded to *Kilmainham Hospital,* very near here; Lord Clarendon going in the carriage with the ladies and myself—Albert and the other gentlemen riding. Sir Edward Blakeney and his staff, and George, received us. We saw the old pensioners, the chapel, and the hall, a fine large room (where all the pensioners dine, as at *Chelsea*), and then Sir Edward's private apartments. We afterwards took a drive through all the principal parts of *Dublin,—College Green,* where the celebrated statue of William the III. is to be seen; *Stephens' Green,* by *The Four*

Courts, a very handsome building; and, though we were not expected, the crowds were in many places very great. We returned a little before seven. A large dinner. After dinner above two or three hundred people arrived, including most of the Irish nobility and many of the gentry; and afterwards there was a ball.

Wednesday, August 8.

At twenty minutes to one o'clock we left for *Dublin*, I and all the ladies in evening dresses, all the gentlemen in uniform. We drove straight to the Castle. Everything here as at *St. James's* Levée. The staircase and throne-room quite like a palace. I received (on the throne) the addresses of the Lord Mayor and Corporation, the University, the Archbishop and Bishops, both Roman Catholic and Anglican, the Presbyterians, the non-subscribing Presbyterians, and the Quakers. They also presented Albert with addresses.* Then followed a very long Levée,

* Lord Breadalbane (Lord Chamberlain) was in attendance, having joined us on our arrival in Dublin.

which lasted without intermission till twenty minutes to six o'clock!· Two thousand people were presented !

Thursday, August 9.

There was a great and brilliant review in the *Phœnix Park*—six thousand one hundred and sixty men, including the Constabulary. In the evening we two dined alone, and at half-past eight o'clock drove into *Dublin* for the Drawing-room. It is always held here of an evening. I should think between two and three thousand people passed before us, and one thousand six hundred ladies were presented. After it was over we walked through *St. Patrick's Hall* and the other rooms, and the crowd was very great. We came back to the *Phœnix Park* at half-past twelve—the streets still densely crowded. The city was illuminated.

Friday, August 10.

At a quarter to twelve o'clock we set out, with all our suite, for *Carton*, the Duke of Leinster's ;

Lord and Lady Clarendon in the carriage with us. We went through *Woodlands*, a place belonging to Mr. White, in which there are beautiful lime-trees; and we passed by the "Preparatory College" for *Maynooth;* and not far from *Carton* we saw a number of the Maynooth students. The park of *Carton* is very fine. We arrived there at a little past one, and were received by the Duke and Duchess of Leinster, the Kildares, Mr. and Lady C. Repton, and their two sons. We walked out into the garden, where all the company were assembled, and the two bands playing; it is very pretty : a sort of formal French garden with rows of Irish yews. We walked round the garden twice, the Duke leading me, and Albert the Duchess. The Duke is one of the kindest, and best of men.

After luncheon we walked out and saw some of the country people dance jigs, which was very amusing. It is quite different from the Scotch reel; not so animated, and the steps different, but very droll. The people were very poorly dressed in thick coats, and the women in shawls. There was one man who was a regular specimen of an Irishman, with his hat on one ear. Others in blue coats, with short breeches and blue stockings. There were three old and tattered pipers playing. The Irish pipe is very different from the Scotch ; it is very weak, and they don't blow into it, but merely have small bellows which they move with the arm. We walked round the pleasure-grounds, and after this got into a carriage with the Duke and Duchess—our ladies and gentlemen following in a large jaunting-car, and the people riding, running, and driving with us, but extremely well-behaved ; and the Duke is so kind to them, that a word from him will make them do anything. It was very hot, and yet the people kept running the whole way, and in the thick woollen coats, which it seems they always wear here. We drove along the park to a spot which commands an extensive view of the *Wicklow Hills*. We then went down an entirely new road, cut out of the solid rock, through a beautiful valley, full of the finest trees, growing among rocks close to a piece of water. We got out and walked across a little wooden bridge to a very pretty little cottage, entirely ornamented with shells, &c. by the Duchess. We drove back in the jaunting-car, which is a double one, with four wheels, and held a number of us—I sitting on one side between Albert and the Duke ; the Duchess, Lady Jocelyn, Lord Clarendon, and Lady Waterford, on the opposite side ; George at the back, and the equerries on either side of the coachman.

As soon as we returned to the house we took leave of our hosts, and went back to the *Phœnix Park* a different way from the one we came, along the banks of the *Liffey*, through Mr. Colson's park, in which there were the most splendid beeches I have ever seen—feathering down quite to the ground ; and farther along the road and river were some lovely sycamore-trees. We drove through the village of *Lucan*, where there were fine decorations and arches of bays and laurel. We passed below *The Strawberry-beds*, which are really curious to see—quite high banks of them—and numbers of people come from *Dublin* to eat these strawberries ; and there are rooms at the bottom of these banks on purpose. We were home a little after five.

On Board the Victoria and Albert,
in Loch Ryan,
Sunday, August 12.

♦We arrived after a dreadfully rough though very short passage, and have taken refuge here. To return to Friday. We left the *Phœnix Park*, where we spent so pleasant a time, at six o'clock, Lord Clarendon and the two elder children going in the carriage with us, and drove with an escort to the Dublin Railway Station. The town was immensely crowded, and the people most enthusiastic. George met us there, and we took him, the Clarendons, and Lord Lansdowne and our ladies in the carriage with us. We arrived speedily at *Kingstown*, where there were just as many people and as much enthusiasm as on the occasion of our disembarkation. We stood on the paddle-box as we slowly steamed out of *Kingstown*, amidst the cheers of thousands and thousands, and salutes from all the ships; and I waved my handkerchief as a parting acknowledgment of their loyalty. We soon passed *Howth* and *Ireland's Eye*. The ship was very steady, though the sea was not smooth, and the night thick and rainy, and we feared a storm was coming on.

Saturday, August 11.

We reached *Belfast Harbour* at four o'clock. The wind had got up amazingly, and the morning was a very bad and stormy one.

We had not had a very quiet night for sleeping, though very smooth. The weather got worse and worse, and blew a real gale; and it was quite doubtful whether we could start as we had intended, on our return from *Belfast*, for *Scotland*.

We saw the Mayor and General (Bainbrigg), who had come on board after breakfast.

At a quarter-past one we started with the ladies and gentlemen for the " Fairy." Though we had only two minutes' row in the barge, there was such a swell that the getting in and out, and the rolling and tossing in the boat, were very disagreeable. We had to keep in the little pavilion, as the squalls were so violent as to cover the " Fairy " with spray. We passed between *Holywood* and *Carrickfergus*, celebrated for the first landing of William III. We reached *Belfast* in half an hour, and fortunately the sun came out.

We lay close alongside the wharf, where a very fine landing-place was arranged, and where thousands were assembled. Lord Londonderry came on board, and numerous deputations with addresses, including the Mayor (whom I knighted), the Protestant Bishop of Down and clergy, the Catholic Bishop Denvir (an excellent and modest man), the Sheriff and Members for the county, with Lord Donegal (to whom the greater part of *Belfast* belongs), Dr. Henry, from the new College, and the Presbyterians (of whom there are a great many here). Lady Londonderry and her daughter also came on board. There was some delay in getting the gang-board down, as they had made much too large a one. Some planks on board were arranged, and we landed easily in this way. The landing-place was covered in, and very tastefully decorated. We got into Lord Londonderry's carriage with the two ladies, and Lord Londonderry himself got on the rumble behind with the two sergeant-footmen, Renwick and Birbage, both very tall, large men; and the three must have been far from comfortable.

The town was beautifully decorated with flowers, hangings, and very fine triumphal arches, the galleries full of people; and the reception very hearty. The people are a mixture of nations, and the female beauty had almost disappeared.

I have all along forgotten to say that the favourite motto written up on most of the arches, &c., and in every place, was: "Cead mile failte," which means "A hundred thousand welcomes" in Irish, which is very like Gaelic; it is in fact *the* language, and has existed in books from the earliest period, whereas Gaelic has only been *written* since half a century, though it was always *spoken*. They often called out, "Cead mile failte!" and it appears in every sort of shape.

Lord Donegal rode on one side of the carriage and the General on the other. We stopped at the *Linen Hall* to see the exhibition of the flax and linen manufacture. Lord Downshire and several other gentlemen received us there, and conducted us through the different rooms, where we saw the whole process in its different stages. First the plant, then the flax after being steeped; then the spun flax; lastly, the linen, cambric, and cloth of every sort and kind. It is really very interesting to see, and it is wonderful to what a state of perfection it has been brought.

We got into our carriages again. This time Lord Londonderry did not attempt to resume his uncomfortable position.

We went along through the *Botanic Garden*, and stopped and got out to look at the new College which is to be opened in October. It is a handsome building. We passed through several of the streets and returned to the place of embarkation. *Belfast* is a fine town, with some good buildings—for instance, the *Bank* and *Exchange*,—and is considered the *Liverpool* and *Manchester* of *Ireland*.

I have forgotten to mention the Constabulary, who are a remarkably fine body of men, 13,000 in number (altogether in *Ireland*), all Irish, and chiefly Roman Catholics ; and not one of whom, during the trying times last year, fraternised with the rebels.

We left amid immense cheering, and reached the " Victoria and Albert" at half-past six. It was blowing as hard as ever, and the getting in and out was as disagreeable as before. We decided on spending the night where we were, unless the wind should drop by three or four o'clock in the morning. Many bonfires were lighted on the surrounding hills and coasts.

Sunday, August 12.

The weather no better, and as there seemed no hope of its improvement, we decided on starting at two o'clock, and proceeding either to *Loch Ryan* or *Lamlash.* Lord Adolphus read the service at half-past ten, at which the two eldest children were also present.

I intend to create Bertie " Earl of Dublin," as a compliment to the town and country; he has no Irish title, though he is *born* with several Scotch ones (belonging to the heirs to the Scotch throne, and which we have inherited from James VI. of Scotland and I. of England); and this was one of my father's titles.

The preparations on deck for the voyage were not encouraging; the boats hoisted up, the accommodation ladders drawn quite close up, every piece of carpet removed, and everything covered; and, indeed, my worst fears were realized. We started at two, and I went below and lay down shortly after, and directly we got out of the harbour the yacht began rolling for the first three-quarters of an hour, in a way which was dreadful, and there were two rolls, when the waves broke over the ship, which I never shall forget. It got gradually better, and at five we entered *Loch Ryan*, truly thankful to be at the end of our voyage. Albert came down to me and then I went up on deck, and he told me how awful it had been. The first great wave which came over the ship threw everybody down in every direction. Poor little Affie* was thrown down and sent rolling over the deck, and was drenched, for the deck was swimming with water. Albert told me it was quite frightful to see the enormous waves rising like a wall above the sides of the ship. We did not anchor so high up in *Loch Ryan* as we had done two years ago ; but it was a very safe quiet anchorage, and we were very glad to be there. Albert went on shore.

Monday, August 13.

We started at four o'clock in the morning, and the yacht rolled a little, but the motion was an easy one. We were in the *Clyde* by breakfast-time, but the day was very bad, constant squalls hiding the scenery. We left *Greenock* to our

* Prince Alfred.

left, and proceeded a little way up *Loch Goil,*
which opens into *Loch Long,* and is very fine;
it seems extraordinary to have such deep water
in a narrow loch and so immediately below the
mountains, which are very rocky. We turned
back and went up *Loch Long,* which I remembered so well, and which is so beautiful. We
let go the anchor at *Arrochar,* the head of the
lake, intending to land and proceed to *Loch
Lomond,* where a steamer was waiting for us;
but it poured with rain most hopelessly. We
waited an hour in vain, and decided on stopping
till after luncheon and making the attempt at three
o'clock. We lunched and stepped into the boat,
as it had cleared a little; but just then it began
pouring again more violently than before, and we
put back much disappointed, but Albert persevered,
and he went off with Mr. Anson, Sir James Clark,
and Captain Robinson almost directly afterwards.
Just then it cleared and I felt so vexed that we
had not gone; but there have been some terrible
showers since. We left *Arrochar* a little before
four, *Loch Long* looking beautiful as we returned.

Perth,
> *Tuesday, August* 14.

We anchored yesterday in *Roseneath Bay*, close to *Roseneath*—a very pretty spot—and looking towards the mountains which you see in *Loch Goil.* One of them is called " The Duke of Argyll's Bowling-green." Albert only returned soon after eight o'clock, having been able to see a good deal of *Loch Lomond,* and even *Rob Roy's Cave,* in spite of heavy showers. Captain Beechey (who was with us during the whole voyage in '47, and again the whole of this one to pilot us), Captain Crispin, and Captain Robinson (who met us this morning and piloted Albert in *Loch Lomond,* and did the same for us in '47), dined with us also, and we had much interesting conversation about the formation of glaciers, &c., in all of which Captain Beechey (who is a very intelligent man, and has been all over the world) took part. He was with Sir Edward Parry at the *North Pole,* and told us that they had not seen daylight for four months. They heaped up snow over the ship and covered it in with boards to keep the cold off.

Balmoral,
Wednesday, August 15.

It seems like a dream to be here in our dear Highland home again; it certainly does not seem as if it were a year since we were here! Now I must describe the doings of yesterday. We embarked on board the " Fairy " at a quarter to nine o'clock, and proceeded up the *Clyde* in pouring rain and high wind, and it was very stormy till after we had passed *Greenock.* We steamed past *Port Glasgow,* then came *Dumbarton* and *Erskine.* The river narrows and winds extraordinarily here, and you do not see *Glasgow* until you are quite close upon it. As we approached, the banks were lined with people, either on estrades or on the sea-shore, and it was amusing to see all those on the shore take flight, often too late, as the water bounded up from the swell caused by the steamer.

The weather, which had been dreadful, cleared up, just as we reached *Glasgow,* about eleven, and continued fine for the remainder of the day. Several addresses were presented on board, first by the Lord Provost, who was knighted, (Colonel Gordon's sword being used,) then one from the county, the clergy (Established Church and Free Kirk), and from the Houses of Commerce. We landed immediately after this; the landing-place was very handsomely decorated. We then entered our carriage with the two eldest children, the two others following. Mr. Alison (the celebrated historian, who is the Sheriff) rode on one side of the carriage, and General Riddell (the Commander of the Forces in Scotland) on the other. The crowds assembled were quite enormous, but excellent order was kept and they were very enthusiastic. Mr. Alison said that there were 500,000 people out. The town is a handsome one with fine streets built in stone, and many fine buildings and churches. We passed over a bridge commanding an extensive view down two quays, which Albert said was very like *Paris.* There are many large shops and warehouses, and the shipping is immense.

We went up to the old cathedral, where Principal Mac Farlane, a very old man, received us, and directed our attention, as we walked through the church gates, to an immensely high chimney, the highest I believe in existence, which belongs to one of the manufactories. The cathedral is a very fine one, the choir of which is fitted up as a Presbyterian church. We were shown the crypt and former burial-place of the bishops, which is in a very high state of preservation. The architecture is beautiful. It is in this crypt that the famous scene in *Rob Roy* is laid, where Rob Roy gives Frank Osbaldistone warning that he is in danger. There is an old monument of St. Kentigern, commonly called St. Mungo, the founder of the cathedral. We re-entered our carriages and went to the *University*, an ancient building, and which has produced many great and learned men. Here we got out and received an address. We only stopped a few minutes, and then went on again towards the *Exchange*, in front of which is Marochetti's equestrian statue of the Duke of Wellington, very like and beautifully executed. We got out at the railway station and started almost immediately.

We passed *Stirling* in the distance, and a little before four we reached *Perth*, where the people were very friendly. We took the four children in our carriage and drove straight to the " George

Inn," where we had the same rooms that we had last time.

Albert went out immediately to see the prison, and at six we drove together along the *London Road* (as they rather strangely call it), towards *Moncrieffe*. The view was perfectly beautiful, and is the finest of *Perth* and the grand bridge over the *Tay*.

Wednesday, August 15.

At a quarter to eight o'clock we started. The two boys and Vicky were in the carriage with us, Alice followed with the ladies. It was a long journey, but through very beautiful scenery. We saw the *Grampians* as we left *Perth*. We first changed horses at *Blairgowrie*, 15 miles. Then came a very long stage of 20 miles, to the *Spittal of Glenshee*. We first passed the house of a Lieut.-Colonel Clark Rattray, called *Craig Hall*, overhanging a valley or glen above which we drove, and after this we came into completely wild Highland scenery, with barren rocky hills, through which the road winds to the *Spittal of Glenshee*, which can scarcely be called a village, for it consists of only an inn and two or three cottages. We got out at the inn, where we found Mr. Farquharson and his son, and some of his men. · Here we had some luncheon, and then set off again. The next stage of 15 miles to *Castleton* is over a very bad, and at night, positively dangerous road, through wild, grand scenery, with very abrupt turns and steep ascents. One sharp turn is called *The Devil's Elbow.* The Farquharson men joined us again here, some having gone on before, and others having followed from the inn, skipping over stones and rocks with the rapidity and lightness peculiar to Highlanders. They remained with us till we were able to trot on again.

We drove through a very fine pass called *Cairn Wall* and were overtaken by a heavy shower. When we reached *Castleton* the day had cleared, and we were able to open the carriage again. Here we were met by Sir Alexander Duff and the Duke of Leeds at the head of their men. Lady Duff, Mr. and Lady Agnes Duff, Miss Farquharson, and several of the children, and the Duchess of Leeds, came up to the carriage. The drive from *Castleton* to *Balmoral*, particularly the beautiful part from the *Balloch Buie*, was well known to us ; and it was a great pleasure to see it all again in its beauty. Grant had met us at the *Spittal of Glenshee*, and ridden the whole way with us. At the door at *Balmoral* were Mackay, who was playing, and Macdonald in full dress. It was about four when we arrived.

YACHTING EXCURSION.

———

On Board the Victoria and Albert,
Dartmouth,
Thursday, August 20, 1846.

We steamed past the various places on the
beautiful coast of *Devonshire* which we had passed
three years ago—*Seaton, Sidmouth,* off which we
stopped for ten minutes, *Axmouth, Teignmouth,*
&c. ;—till we came to *Babbicombe,* a small bay,
where we remained an hour. It is a beautiful
spot, which before we had only passed at a distance. Red cliffs and rocks with wooded hills
like *Italy,* and reminding one of a ballet or play
where nymphs are to appear—such rocks and
grottos, with the deepest sea, on which there was
not a ripple. We intended to disembark and
walk up the hill ; but it came on to rain very

much, and we could not do so. We tried to sketch the part looking towards *Torbay*. I never saw our good children looking better, or in higher spirits. I contrived to give Vicky a little lesson, by making her read in her English history.

We proceeded on our course again at half past one o'clock, and saw *Torquay* very plainly, which is very fine. The sea looked so stormy and the weather became so thick that it was thought best to give up *Plymouth* (for the third time), and to put into that beautiful *Dartmouth*, and we accordingly did so, in pouring rain, the deck swimming with water, and all of us with umbrellas ; the children being most anxious to see everything. Notwithstanding the rain, this place is lovely, with its wooded rocks and church and castle at the entrance. It puts me much in mind of the beautiful *Rhine*, and its fine ruined castles, and the *Lurlei*.

I am now below writing, and crowds of boats are surrounding us on all sides.

Plymouth Harbour,
Friday, August 21.

We got under weigh by half-past six o'clock, and on looking out we saw the sea so calm and blue and the sun so bright that we determined to get up. It was a very fine day, but there was a great deal of swell. At length at half-past nine we entered the splendid harbour of *Plymouth*, and anchored again below *Mount Edgcumbe;* which, with its beautiful trees, including pines, growing down into the sea, looks more lovely than ever. I changed my dress and read innumerable letters and despatches, and then went on deck and saw the authorities—the Admirals and Generals. I did Vicky's lessons and wrote; and at half-past one we went on board the " Fairy," (leaving the children on board the " Victoria and Albert,") with all our ladies and gentlemen, as well as Sir James Clark, who has joined us here. We steamed up the *Tamar,* going first a little way up the *St. Germans* river, which has very prettily wooded banks. *Trematon Castle* to the right, which belongs to Bertie as Duke of Cornwall, and *Jats* to the left, are ex-

tremely pretty. We stopped here and afterwards
turned back and went up the *Tamar*, which at
first seemed flat ; but as we proceeded the scenery
became quite beautiful—richly wooded hills, the
trees growing down into the water, and the river
winding so much as to have the effect of a lake.
In this it reminded me so much of going up the
Rhine,—though I don't think the river resembles
the *Rhine*. Albert thought it like the *Danube*.
The finest parts begin about *Saltash*, which is a
small but prettily built town. To the right as
you go up all is un-English looking ; a little
farther on is the mouth of the *Tavy ;* here the
river becomes very beautiful. We passed numbers
of mines at work. Further on, to the left, we
came to *Pentillie Castle* situated on a height most
beautifully wooded down to the water's edge, and
the river winding rapidly above and below it.
Albert said it reminded him of the situation of
Greinburg on the *Danube*. Not much further on we
came to the picturesque little village and landing-
place of *Cothele*, at the foot of a thickly wooded
bank, with a valley on one side. Here the river
is very narrow. We landed, and drove up a steep
hill under fine trees to the very curious old

House of Cothelc, where we got out of the carriage. It is most curious in every way—as it stands in the same state as it was in the time of Henry VII. and is in great preservation—the old rooms hung with arras, &c.

We drove down another way under beautiful trees and above the fine valley; embarked and proceeded down the river. The evening was beautiful, the sun bright, and the sky and sea so blue. We arrived just too late for the launch of the frigate "Thetis." It reminded me so much of when we were here three years ago, as we approached our yacht, surrounded by myriads of boats, and had to row through them in our barge. We returned at half-past five. The evening was delightful—clear, calm, and cloudless, but a good deal of noise in the boats around us. Lord and Lady Mount Edgcumbe and Sir James Clark dined with us.

Plymouth,
Saturday, August 22.

Albert was up at six o'clock, as he was to go to *Dartmoor Forest*. At ten I went in the barge with the two children, the ladies, Baron Stockmar, and Lord Alfred Paget, and landed at *Mount Edgcumbe*, where we were received by Lady Mount Edgcumbe, her two boys, her sister and nieces, and beyond the landing-place by Lord Mount Edgcumbe. There were crowds where we landed, and I feel so shy and put out without Albert. I got into a carriage with the children and Lady Mount Edgcumbe — Lord Mount Edgcumbe going before us and the others following—and took a lovely drive along the road which overhangs the bay, commanding such beautiful views on all sides, and going under and by such fine trees. We had been there three years ago ; but it is always a pleasure to see it again. The day very hot and a little hazy. We came to the house at eleven. The children went with their governess and the other children into the shade and had luncheon in the house, and I remained in the gallery—a very pretty room, with some fine pictures, and with a door opening on the garden, and commanding a lovely little bit of sea view, which I tried to sketch. A little after twelve we returned to the yacht, which had been beset with boats ever since six in the morning. Albert returned safely to me at one o'clock, much pleased with his trip; and said that *Dartmoor Forest* was like *Scotland.*

At two we went with our ladies and gentlemen, and without the children, again to the landing-place at *Mount Edgcumbe,* where we were received as before, and drove up to the house. There are some of the finest and tallest chestnut-trees in existence here, and the beech-trees grow very peculiarly—quite tall and straight —the branches growing upwards. We walked about the gallery and looked into Lady Mount Edgcumbe's little room at one end of it, which is charming, and full of pretty little things which she has collected, and then we took luncheon in a room where there are some fine portraits by Sir Joshua Reynolds. They are all of the Mount Edgcumbe family, one of whom was his great patron. Sir Joshua was born a few miles from *Plymouth.* There are in the same room pictures by him when he first began to paint, which have kept their colour; then when he made experiments—and these are quite faded; and again of his works when he discovered his mistakes, and the colour of his pictures is then beautiful. We walked about the garden near the house, and then drove to the "Kiosk," by beautiful stone pines and pinasters, which interested Albert very much, and put me so much in mind of Mr. Lear's drawings. The view from this "Kiosk," which is very high over the sea and town, is most beautiful, and the sea was like glass, not a ripple to be seen. We walked down a very pretty road or path through the woods and trees till we met the carriage, and we drove along that beautiful road, which is said to be a little like the *Cornice*, overhanging the sea, down to the place of embarkation, where we took leave of them all, and returned to our yacht by half-past four. Poor Lord Mount Edgcumbe is in such a sad, helpless state; but so patient and cheerful. We went on board just to fetch the children, and then on to the "Fairy," and steamed in her round the harbour, or rather bay, in which there are such pretty spots; into the *Cat Water*, from whence we rowed in one of the barges a little way up the river to look at *Saltram*, Lord Morley's; after that back to the "Fairy," went in her into *Mill Bay, Sutton Pool*, and *Stone-house*, and returned to the yacht by half-past six.

In Guernsey Bay, off St. Pierre, Guernsey,
Sunday, August 23.

On waking, the morning was so lovely that we could not help regretting that we could not delay our trip a little, by one day at least, as the Council which was to have been on the 25th is now on the 29th. We thought, however, we could do nothing but sail for *Torbay*, at half-past nine, and for *Osborne* on Monday. While dressing, I kept thinking whether we could not manage to see *Falmouth*, or something or other. Albert thought we might perhaps manage to see one of the *Channel Islands*, and accordingly he sent for Lord Adolphus Fitzclarence, and it was settled that we should go to *Guernsey*, which delighted me, as I had so long wished to see it. The day splendid. The General and Admiral came on board to take leave. Sir J. West is the Admiral, and

General Murray, the General; and at about half-past nine we set off, and the sea the whole way was as calm as it was in '43. *Plymouth* is beautiful, and we shall always be delighted to return there.

For two hours we were in expectation of seeing land; but it was very hazy, and they did not know where we were—till about six, when land was seen by the "Fairy," who came to report it, and then all the other vessels went on before us. As we approached we were struck by the beauty of the *Guernsey* coast, in which there are several rocky bays, and the town of *St. Pierre* is very picturesquely built, down to the water's edge. You see *Sark* (or *Sercq*) as you enter the harbour to the right, and further on, close opposite *St. Pierre*, two islands close together—*Herm* and *Jethou*. The bay with these fine islands is really most curious. We anchored at seven, immediately opposite *St. Pierre*, and with the two islands on the other side of us. We dined at eight, and found on going on deck the whole town illuminated, which had a very pretty effect, and must have been done very quickly, for they had no idea of our coming. It is built like a foreign town. The people speak mostly French amongst themselves.

August 24.

St. Pierre is very picturesque-looking — with very high, bright-coloured houses built down almost into the sea. The College and Church are very conspicuous buildings. This island with its bold point, and the little one of *Cornet* with a sort of castle on it (close to which we were anchored), and the three islands of *Herm, Jethou,* and *Sark,* with innumerable rocks, are really very fine and peculiar,—especially as they then were in bright sunlight. We both sketched, and at a quarter to nine got into our barge with our ladies. The pier and shore were lined with crowds of people, and with ladies dressed in white, singing " God save ' the Queen," and strewing the ground with flowers. We walked to our carriage, preceded by General Napier, brother to Sir Charles (in *Scinde*), a very singular-looking old man, tall and thin, with an aquiline nose, piercing eyes, and white moustaches and hair. The people were extremely well-behaved and friendly, and received us very warmly as we drove through the narrow streets, which were decorated with flowers and flags, and lined with the *Guernsey* militia, 2,000 strong, with their several bands. Some of the militia were mounted.

The vegetation beyond the town is exceedingly fine ; and the evergreens and flowers most abundant. The streets and hills steep, and the view from the fort, which is very high, (and where General Napier presented me with the keys,) is extremely beautiful. You look over the bay of *Guernsey*, and see opposite to you the islands of *Herm*, *Jethou*, and *Sark ;* with *Alderney*, and the coast of *France*, *Cape de la Hague*, to the left in the distance, and to the right in the distance, *Jersey*. The island appears very flourishing. In the town they speak English, but in the country French, and this is the same in all the 'islands. They belonged to the Duchy of Normandy, and have been in our possession ever since William the Conqueror's time. King John was the last of their sovereigns who visited them. We drove along the pier, and then embarked amidst great cheering. It was all admirably managed ; the people are extremely loyal.

We got under weigh a little before one and

in about an hour-and-a-half we came close to *Alderney*, seeing all the time the French coast, *Cape de la Hague*, very plainly to our right, and leaving the *Casquets Lights* to our left. *Alderney* is quite different from all the other islands, excessively rocky and barren, and the rocks in and under the sea are most frightful.

SECOND YACHTING EXCURSION.

————

On Board the Victoria and Albert,
Off St. Heliers, Jersey,
Wednesday, September 2, 1846.

At a quarter-past seven o'clock we set off with Vicky, Bertie, Lady Jocelyn, Miss Kerr, Mdlle. Gruner, Lord Spencer, Lord Palmerston, and Sir James Clark (Mr. Anson and Colonel Grey being on board the " Black Eagle "), and embarked at *Osborne Pier.* There was a good deal of swell. It was fine, but very cold at first. At twelve we saw *Alderney,* and between two and three got into the *Alderney Race,* where there was a great deal of rolling, but not for long. We passed between *Alderney* and the French coast—*Cape de la Hague*—and saw the other side of *Alderney;* and then, later, *Sark, Guernsey,* and the other islands. After passing the *Alderney*

Race it became quite smooth; and then Bertie put on his sailor's dress, which was beautifully made by the man on board who makes for our sailors. When he appeared, the officers and sailors, who were all assembled on deck to see him, cheered, and seemed delighted with him.

The coast of *Jersey* is very beautiful, and we had to go nearly all round, in order to get to *St. Heliers.* We first passed the point called *Rondnez,* then *Grosnez* with a tower, *St. Ouen's Bay, La Rocca,* a curious old tower on a rock, and then *Brelade's Bay.* The red cliffs and rocks, with the setting sun gilding and lighting them all up, were beautiful. At last, at a quarter to seven, we arrived in this fine large bay of *St. Aubin,* in which lies *St. Heliers;* and after dinner we went on deck to see the illumination and the bonfires.

Off St. Helicrs,
  Thursday, September 3.

A splendid day. I never saw a more beautiful deep blue sea, quite like *Naples ;* and Albert said that this fine bay of *St. Aubin,* in which we lie, really is like *Naples. Noirmont Point* terminates in a low tower to our left, with *St. Aubin* and a tower on a rock in front of it; farther in, and to our right, *Elizabeth Castle,* a picturesque fort on a rock, with the town of *St. Helicrs* behind it.

The colouring and the effect of light were indescribably beautiful. We got into our barge with our ladies and gentlemen, and then went on board the "Fairy," until we were close to the harbour, and then we got into the barge again. We landed at the stairs of the *Victoria Harbour,* amid the cheers of the numberless crowds, guns firing, and bands playing ; were received, as at *Guernsey,* by all the ladies of the town, very gaily dressed, who, strewing flowers on our way, conducted us to a canopy, where I received the address of the States and of the militia.

We then got into our carriage and drove along the pier; Colonel Le Couteur, my militia aide-de-camp, riding by my side, with other officers, and by Albert's side Colonel Le Breton, commanding the militia, who, 5,000 strong, lined the streets, and were stationed along the pier. The States walking in front. The crowds were immense, but everything in excellent order, and the people most enthusiastic, though not more so than the good *Guernsey* people; the town is much larger, and they had much longer time for preparations; the decorations and arches of flowers were really beautifully done, and there were numberless kind inscriptions. All the country people here speak French, and so did the police who walked near us. It was a very gratifying reception. There was a seat in one of the streets filled by Frenchwomen from *Granville*, curiously dressed with white handkerchiefs on their heads. After passing through several streets we drove up to the *Government House*, but did not get out. General Gibbs, the Governor, is very infirm.

We then proceeded at a quicker pace— the walking procession having ceased—through the interior of the island, which is extremely pretty and very green,—orchards without end, as at *Mayence.* We passed the curious old tower of *La Hougue Bie,* of very ancient date, and went to the *Castle of Mont Orgueil,* in *Grouville Bay,* very beautifully situated, completely over-hanging the sea, and where Robert, Duke of Normandy, son of William the Conqueror, is said to have lived. We walked part of the way up, and from one of the batteries, where no guns are now mounted, you command the bay, and the French coast is distinctly seen, only 13 miles distant. The people are very proud that *Mont Orgueil* had never been taken; but I have since learnt it was taken by surprise and held for a few days; *Guernsey,* however, *never* was taken.

We then returned to our carriage, and pro-ceeded to the pier by a shorter road, and through a different part of the town. There is a peculiar elm-tree in the island, which is very pretty, and unlike any other,—the leaf and the way it grows almost resembling the acacia. The crowd was very great and the heat very intense in going back.

We re-embarked in the barge, but had only to go a few yards to the " Fairy." The situation of the harbour is very fine,—and crowned with the fort, and covered by numbers of people, was like an amphitheatre. The heat of the sun, and the glare, had made me so ill and giddy that I remained below the greater part of the afternoon, and Albert went out for an hour on the "Fairy."

Falmouth Harbour,
Friday, Sept. 4.

A beautiful day again, with the same brilliantly blue sea. At a quarter to eight o'clock we got under weigh. There was a great deal of motion at first, and for the greater part of the day the ship pitched, but getting up the sails steadied her. From five o'clock it became quite smooth; at half-past five we saw land, and at seven we entered *Falmouth Harbour*, where we were immediately surrounded by boats. The evening was beautiful and the sea as smooth as glass, and without even a ripple. The calmest night possible, with a beautiful moon, when we went on deck; every now and then the splashing of oars and the hum of voices were heard; but they were the only sounds, unlike the constant dashing of the sea against the vessel, which we heard all the time we were at *Jersey*.

Mount's Bay, Cornwall,
Saturday, September 5.

At eight o'clock we left *Falmouth* and proceeded along the coast of *Cornwall*, which becomes
bold and rugged beyond the *Lizard Point* and
as one approaches *Land's End.* At about twelve
we passed *Land's End*, which is very fine and
rocky, the view from thence opening beautifully.
We passed quite close by the *Longships*, some
rocks on which stands a lighthouse. The sea
was unusually smooth for the *Land's End.* We
went beyond a point with some rocks near it,
called *The Brisons*, and then steamed back ; the
famous Botallack mine lies here. A little before
two we landed in this beautiful *Mount's Bay*,
close below *St. Michael's Mount*, which is very
fine. When the bay first opened to our view the
sun was lighting up this beautiful castle, so peculiarly built on a lofty rock, and which forms an
island at high water.

In entering the bay we passed the small village
of *Mousehole* and the town of *Penzance*, which is
prettily situated, about one mile and a half from

St. Michael's Mount.   The day brightened just as we arrived, and the sea again became so blue.

Soon after our arrival we anchored; the crowd of boats was beyond everything; numbers of Cornish pilcher fishermen, in their curious large boats, kept going round and round, and then anchored, besides many other boats full of people.   They are a very noisy, talkative race, and speak a kind of English hardly to be understood.

During our voyage I was able to give Vicky her lessons.   At three o'clock we all got into the barge, including the children and Mdlle. Gruner, their governess, and rowed through an avenue of boats of all descriptions to the " Fairy," where we went on board.   The getting in and out of the barge was no easy task.   There was a good deal of swell, and the " Fairy" herself rolled amazingly. We steamed round the bay to look at *St. Michael's*

Mount from the other side, which is even more beautiful, and then went on to *Penzance*. Albert landed near *Penzance* with all the gentlemen, except Lord Spencer (who is most agreeable, efficient, and useful at sea, being a Captain of the Navy) and Colonel Grey, and went to see the smelting of copper and tin, and the works in serpentine stone at *Penzance*. We remained here a little while without going on, in order to sketch, and returned to the " Victoria and Albert" by half-past four, the boats crowding round us in all directions; and when Bertie showed himself the people shouted :—" Three cheers for the Duke of Cornwall !" Albert returned a little before seven, much gratified by what he had seen, and bringing home specimens of the serpentine stone.

Mount's Bay.
Sunday, September 6.

A hazy, dull-looking morning, but as calm as it possibly could be. At half-past eight o'clock we got into our barge, with Miss Kerr and Lord Spencer, and proceeded without any standard to the little harbour below *St. Michael's Mount.*

Behind *St. Michael's Mount* is the little town of
Marazion, or "Market Jew," which is supposed
to have taken its name from the Jews having
in former times trafficked there. We disembarked and walked up the *Mount* by a circuitous
rugged path over rocks and turf, and entered the
old castle, which is beautifully kept, and must be
a nice house to live in; as there are so many good
rooms in it. The dining-room, made out of the re-
fectory, is very pretty; it is surrounded by a frieze,
representing ancient hunting. The chapel is excessively curious. The organ is much famed;
Albert played a little on it, and it sounded very
fine. Below the chapel is a dungeon, where some
years ago was discovered the skeleton of a large
man without a coffin; the entrance is in the floor
of one of the pews. Albert went down with
Lord Spencer, and afterwards went up with him
and Sir James Clark (who, with Lord Palmerston
and Colonel Grey, had joined us,) to the tower, on
the top of which is "St. Michael's chair," which, it
is said, betrothed couples run up to, and whoever
gets first into the chair will have at home the
government of the house; and the old house-
keeper—a nice tidy old woman—said many a

couple " does go there ! " though Albert and Lord Spencer said it was the awkwardest place possible to get at. *St. Michael's Mount* belongs to Sir J. St. Aubyn. There were several drawings there of *Mont St. Michel* in *Normandy*, which is very like this one; and was, I believe, inhabited by the same order of monks as this was, *i.e.* Benedictines. We walked down again, had to step, over another boat in order to get into our barge, as the tide was so very low, and returned on board the yacht before ten.

The view from the top of *St. Michael's* is very beautiful and very extensive, but unfortunately it was too thick and hazy to see it well. A low ridge of sand separates *St. Michael's Mount* from *Marazion* at low water, and the sea at high water. From the sand to the summit of the castle is about 250 feet. The chapel was originally erected, they say, for the use of pilgrims who came here; and it owes its name to a tradition of St. Michael the Archangel having rested on the rock.

At half-past eleven Lord Spencer read on deck the short morning service generally read at sea, which only lasted twenty or twenty-five minutes. The awning was put up, and flags on the sides;

and all the officers and sailors were there, as well as ourselves. A flag was hoisted, as is usual when the service is performed on board ship, and Lord Spencer read extremely well.

Albert made a most beautiful little sketch of *St. Michael's Mount*. Soon after two we left *Mount's Bay*. About four we came opposite to some very curious serpentine rocks, between *Mount's Bay* and *Lizard Point*, and we stopped, that Albert might land. The gentlemen went with him. Lord Spencer soon returned, saying that Albert was very anxious I should see the beautiful little cave in these serpentine rocks; and accordingly I got into the barge, with the children, and ladies, and Lord Spencer, and we rowed to these rocks, with their caves and little creeks. There were many cormorants and sea-gulls on the rocks. We returned again, and were soon joined by Albert, who brought many fine specimens which he had picked up. The stone is really beautifully marked with red and green veins.

We proceeded on our course, and reached *Falmouth* before seven. The fine afternoon was changed to a foggy, dull, cold evening. We have had on board with us, since we left *Falmouth*, Mr. Taylor, mineral agent to the Duchy of Cornwall, a very intelligent young man, married to a niece of Sir Charles Lemon's.

Falmouth, Monday, September 7.

Immediately after breakfast, Albert left me to land and visit some mines. The corporation of *Penryn* were on board, and very anxious to see "The Duke of Cornwall," so I stepped out of the pavilion on deck with Bertie, and Lord Palmerston told them that that was "The Duke of Cornwall;" and the old mayor of *Penryn* said that "he hoped he would grow up a blessing to his parents and to his country."

A little before four o'clock, we all got into the barge, with the two children, and rowed to the "Fairy." We rowed through a literal *lane* of boats, full of people, who had surrounded the yacht ever since early in the morning, and proceeded up the river by *St. Just's Pool*, to the left of which lies Sir C. Lemon's place, and *Trefusis* belonging to Lord Clinton. We went up the *Truro*, which is beautiful,—something like the *Tamar*, but almost finer, though not so bold as *Pentillie Castle* and *Cothele*,—winding between banks entirely wooded with stunted oak, and full of numberless creeks. The prettiest are *King Harry's Ferry* and a spot near *Tregothnan* (Lord Falmouth's), where there is a beautiful little boat-house, quite in the woods, and on the river, at the point where the *Tregony* separates from the *Truro*. Albert said the position of this boat-house put him in mind of Tell's Chapel in *Switzerland*. We went a little way up the *Tregony*, which is most beautiful, with high sloping banks, thickly wooded down to the water's edge. Then we turned back and went up the *Truro* to *Malpas*, another bend of the river, from whence one can see *Truro*, the capital of *Cornwall*. We stopped here awhile, as so many boats came out from a little place called *Sunny Corner*, just below *Truro*, in order to see us; indeed the whole population poured out on foot and in carts, &c. along the banks; and cheered, and were enchanted when Bertie was held up for them to see. It was a very pretty, gratifying sight.

We went straight on to *Swan Pool* outside *Pendennis Castle*, where we got into the barge, and rowed near to the shore to see a net drawn.

Mr. Fox, a Quaker, who lives at *Falmouth*, and has sent us flowers, fruit, and many other things, proposed to put in his net and draw, that we might see all sorts of fish caught, but when it was drawn there was not one fish! So we went back to the "Fairy." The water near the shore in *Swan Pool* is so wonderfully clear that one could count the pebbles.

Tuesday, September 8.

A wet morning when we rose and breakfasted with the children. At about ten o'clock we entered *Fowey*, which is situated in a creek much like *Dartmouth*, only not so beautiful, but still very pretty. We got into the barge (leaving the children on board, and also Lord Spencer, who was not quite well), and landed at *Fowey* with our ladies and gentlemen, and Mr. Taylor, whom we had brought with us from *Falmouth*. We got into our carriage with the ladies, the gentlemen following in others, and drove through some of the narrowest streets I ever saw in *England*, and up perpendicular hills in the streets—it really quite alarmed one; but we got up and through them quite safely. We then drove on for a long way, on bad and narrow roads, higher and higher up, commanding a fine and very extensive view of the very hilly country of *Cornwall*, its hills covered with fields, and intersected by hedges. At last we came to one field where there was no road whatever, but we went down the hill quite safely, and got out of the carriage at the top of another, where, surrounded by woods, stands a circular ruin, covered with ivy, of the old castle of *Restormel*, belonging to the Duchy of Cornwall, and in which the last Earl of Cornwall lived in the thirteenth century. It was very picturesque from this point.

We visited here the Restormel mine, belonging also to the Duchy of Cornwall. It is an iron mine, and you go in on a level. Albert and I got into one of the trucks and were dragged in by miners, Mr. Taylor walking behind us. The miners wear a curious woollen dress, with a cap like this :  and the dress thus :

and they generally have a candle stuck in front of the cap. This time candlesticks were stuck along the sides of the mine, and those who did not drag or push the truck carried lights. Albert and the gentlemen wore miners' hats. There was no room for any one to pass between the trucks and the rock, and only just room enough to hold up one's head, and not always that. It had a most curious effect, and there was something unearthly about this lit-up cavern-like place. We got out and scrambled a little way to see the veins of ore, and Albert knocked off some pieces; but in general it is blown by gunpowder, being so hard. The miners seemed so pleased at seeing us, and are intelligent, good people. It was quite dazzling when we came into daylight again.

We then got into our carriage and passed through the small town of *Lostwithiel*, where an address was presented to us, and then we passed through Mr. Agar Robarts' Park, which reminded one of *Cothele*. We returned by the same road till near *Fowey*, when we went through some of the narrowest lanes I almost ever drove through, and so fearfully stony. We drove along high above the river to *Place*, belonging to Mr.

Treffry, which has been restored according to drawings in his possession, representing the house as it was in former times. A lady of that name defended the house against the French during the absence of her husband, in the fourteenth or fifteenth century. The old gentleman showed us all over the house, and into an unfinished hall, lined with marble and porphyry, all of which came from *Cornwall.* We then walked down to the place of embarkation and proceeded at once to the yacht. Mr. Taylor deserved the greatest credit for all the arrangements. He and his father are what are called " Adventurers " of the mine.

Osborne,
Wednesday, September 9.

We got up about seven o'clock and found **we** had just passed *The Needles.*

VISIT TO THE LAKES OF KILLARNEY.

Tuesday, August 27, 1861.

At eleven o'clock we all started in our own sociable, and another of our carriages, and on ponies, for *Ross Castle*, the old ruin which was a celebrated stronghold, and from which the Kenmare family take their name. Here there was an immense crowd and a great many boats. We got into a very handsome barge of eight oars —beautifully rowed. Lord Castlerosse steering. The four children, and Lady Churchill, Lady Castlerosse, and Lord Granville were with us.

We rowed first round *Innisfallen Island* and some way up the *Lower Lake*. The view was magnificent. We had a slight shower, which alarmed us all, from the mist which overhung the mountains; but it suddenly cleared away and became very fine and very hot. At a quarter to one we landed at the foot of the beautiful hill of *Glena*, where on a small sloping lawn there is a very pretty little cottage. We walked about, though it was overpoweringly hot, to see some of the splendid views. The trees are beautiful,—oak, birch, arbutus, holly, yew,—all growing down to the water's edge, intermixed with heather. The hills, rising abruptly from the lake, are completely wooded, which gives them a different character from those in *Scotland*, though they often reminded me of the dear *Highlands*. We returned to the little cottage, where the quantity of midges and the smell of peat made us think of *Alt-na-Giuthasach*. Upstairs, from Lady Castlerosse's little room, the view was towards a part of the *Lower Lake*, the outline of which is rather low. We lunched, and afterwards re-embarked, and then took that most beautiful row up the rapid, under the *Old Weir Bridge*, through the channel which connects the two lakes, and which is very intricate and narrow. Close to our right as we were going, we stopped under the splendid hill of the *Eagle's Nest* to hear the *echo* of a bugle; the sound of which, though blown near by, was not heard. We had to get out near the *Weir*

Bridge to let the empty boats be pulled up by the men. The sun had come out and lit up the really magnificent scenery splendidly; but it was most oppressively hot. We wound along till we entered the *Upper Lake*, which opened upon us with all its high hills—the highest, *The Reeks*, 3,400 feet high—and its islands and points covered with splendid trees;—such arbutus (quite large trees) with yews, making a beautiful foreground. We turned into a small bay or creek, where we got out and walked a short way in the shade, and up to where a tent was placed, just opposite a waterfall called *Derricaunihy*, a lovely spot, but terribly infested by midges. In this tent was tea, fruit, ice, cakes, and everything most tastefully arranged. We just took some tea, which was very refreshing in the great heat of this relaxing climate. The vegetation is quite that of a jungle—ferns of all kinds and shrubs and trees,—all springing up luxuriantly. We entered our boats and went back the same way we came, admiring greatly the beauty of the scenery; and this time went down the rapids in the boat. No boats, except our own, had followed us beyond the rapids. But below them there were a great many, and the scene was very animated and the people very noisy and enthusiastic. The Irish always give that peculiar shrill shriek—unlike anything one ever hears anywhere else.

Wednesday, August 28.

At a quarter-past eleven we started on a most beautiful drive, of which I annex the route. We drove with Mrs. Herbert and Bertie in our sociable, driven from the box by Wagland ; * and, though the highest mountains were unfortunately occasionally enveloped in mist, and we had slight showers, we were enchanted with the extreme beauty of the scenery. The peeps of the lake ; the splendid woods full of the most magnificent arbutus, which in one place form, for a few yards,

---

* My coachman since 1857 ; and a good, zealous servant. He entered the Royal service in 1831, and rode as postilion for seventeen years. His father has been thirty-two years porter in the Royal Mews at Windsor, and is now seventy-five years old ; and has been sixty years in the service. His grandfather was also in the Royal service, having entered it in 1788 ; and his daughter is nursery-maid to the Prince of Wales's children. Four generations, therefore, have served the Royal Family.

an avenue under which you drive, with the rocks,
—which are very peculiar—all made it one of the
finest drives we had ever taken. Turning up by
the village and going round, the *Torc* mountain reminded us of *Scotland*—of the woods above
Abergeldie, of *Craig Daign* and *Craig Clunie*. It
was *so* fine. We got out at the top of the *Torc*
Waterfall and walked down to the foot of it. We
came home at half-past one. At four we started
for the boats, quite close by. The *Muckross*
Lake is extremely beautiful; at the beginning
of our expedition it looked dark and severe in
the mist and showers which kept coming on,
just as it does in the *Highlands*. Mr. Herbert steered. Our girls, Mrs. Herbert, Lady
Churchill, and Lord Granville were in the boat
with us. The two boys went in a boat rowed
by gentlemen, and the rest in two other boats.
At Mr. and Mrs. Herbert's request I christened
one of the points which runs into the lake with
a bottle of wine, Albert holding my arm when
we came close by, so that it was most successfully
smashed.

When we emerged from under *Brickeen Bridge*
we had a fine view of the *Lower Lake* and of the

scenery of yesterday, which rather puzzled me, seeing it from another *point de vue*. At *Benson's Point* we stopped for some time, merely rowing about backwards and forwards, or remaining stationary, watching for the deer (all this is a deer forest as well as at *Glena*), which we expected the dogs would find and bring down into the water. But in vain : we waited till past six and no deer came. The evening had completely cleared and became quite beautiful ; and the effect of the numbers of boats full of people, many with little flags, rowing about in every direction and cheering and shouting, lit up by the evening light, was charming. At *Darby's Garden* the shore was densely crowded, and many of the women in their blue cloaks waded into the water, holding their clothes up to their knees.

We were home by seven o'clock, having again a slight sprinkling of rain.

LONDON:

PRINTED BY SMITH, ELDER AND CO.

Lightning Source UK Ltd.
Milton Keynes UK
UKHW020022100223
416721UK00002B/290